How to
Reach
Secular
People

"For years to come this will be the manual for preparing practitioners of evangelism in the western world."
—John R. Hendrick
Professor of Mission and Evangelism
Austin Presbyterian Theological Seminary

"A powerful and compelling guide to understanding and engaging secular people. The emerging opportunity facing the church is not only spelled out, but practical handles are given concerning how that opportunity might be realized."
—Win Arn
Church Growth, Inc.

"Positive directives the Church can follow to reclaim our civilization for Christ."
—William H. Hinson
Pastor, First United Methodist Church, Houston, TX

"This book should be required reading for everyone who wants to communicate the gospel effectively to unchurched persons."
—Robert H. Schuller
Founder, The Crystal Cathedral

How to Reach Secular People

George G. Hunter III

ABINGDON PRESS
Nashville

HOW TO REACH SECULAR PEOPLE

Copyright © 1992 by Abingdon Press

This book is printed on recycled, acid-free paper.

Library of Congress Cataloging-in-Publication Data

HUNTER, GEORGE G.
　　How to reach secular people / George G. Hunter III.
　　　　p.　　cm.
　　Includes bibliographical references and index.
　　ISBN 0-687-17930-0 (alk. paper)
　　1. Evangelistic work. 2. Secularism. I. Title.
BV3790.H893　　　1992
269′ .2—dc20　　　　　　　　　　　　　　　　　　91-28451
　　　　　　　　　　　　　　　　　　　　　　　　CIP

Unless otherwise noted, Scripture quotations are from the New Revised Standard Version of the Bible, © copyright 1989 by the Division of Christian Education of the National Council of Churches of Christ in the United States of America.

The author acknowledges written permission to cite material obtained from private interviews with the following sources: Kenneth L. Chafin, Bill Hybels, Bruce Larson, Donald Morgan, Robert H. Schuller, Donald Soper, Lee Strobel, and Rick Warren. Portions of these interviews are quoted without formal citation about time and place in the book. In addition, permission was obtained to reproduce poetry from William and Catherine Booth, "God's Soldiers (Jenty Fairbank)," © Salvationist Publishing and Supplies Ltd, Kings Cross London, England. Used by permission. Some excerpts are printed from the book, *The Reluctant Witness* by Kenneth Chafin, © 1974 by Broadman Press. Used by Permission. Excerpts from *I Stand By the Door: The Life of Sam Shoemaker* by Helen Smith Shoemaker Copyright © 1967 by Helen Smith Shoemaker. Reprinted by permission of Harper Collins Publishers.

MANUFACTURED IN THE UNITED STATES OF AMERICA

To the Reverend Orville Nelson

*—under whom I answered the
call to communicate the gospel
to nonchristian people.*

To Doctor Lawrence Lacour

*—who first persuaded me
that communication theory could
help the Church communicate the
gospel more effectively.*

C O N T E N T S

F O R E W O R D

---

*T*he title of this treatise is not only self-explanatory but significant. It represents the supreme opportunity and problem of salvation. The theme is the christian gospel. As a fellow practitioner with Dr. Hunter in witnessing to this all-important commitment, I take it as a privilege that I am able to write this foreword.

I can heartily commend what follows on these pages, not least because I can verify out of my own experience the substance of the problems he faces and, above all, the answers he propounds. Here is a comprehensive inquiry, and it is comprehensive in both senses of the word. The assembly of information in which he sets his thesis covers the widest of relevant issues in explication of the general theme. The author's scholarship is indeed comprehensive. It covers the ground.

At the same time that scholarship is critical in the best sense of the word. He understands what he is writing about, and over and over again I have found his judgment impeccable. If truth is the proper selection of evidence, then I find these pages full of intellectual honesty, and that is not always an ingredient in professed evangelism, let alone advocacy. At the same time the author deliberately chooses to identify ''secular people'' as the appropriate phrase in which to specify and diagnose the characteristics of an effective communication of the christian faith.

It is all too fatally easy to assume that an eternal truth is automatically translatable in a changing world. I hold, as he does, that fundamentally the christian faith is relevant whatever the vagaries of circumstance and time. On the other hand to ignore the manifold differences of outlook and circumstance which have crowded in on modern people is as fatal for evangelism as it is for politics and economics.

The communicator, if he or she is to be heard, must begin with the listener where the listener is, and not where the evangelist thinks he or she ought to be. Thus the author has very wisely chosen the adjective *secular* to describe people today. Whatever its original meaning, the word *secular* describes preoccupation with human affairs often to the exclusion of eternal well-being. It fills the mind with passing events, and it acquaints men and women today with a plethora of so-called information about this planet of which our ancestors knew precious little. It includes the vastly increased powers that science puts into our hands whereby morals intertwine with circumstance. "Nuclear energy" is the shorthand with which to describe our human capacity to change what hitherto was unchangeable at least by human hands. Doctor Hunter is not stranger to these and many more facts of a nuclear age which in so many respects is unprecedented. Daunting as these matters are, the presentation of the eternal gospel must be set within their framework, and the author does just that.

I commend *How to Reach Secular People*. I would presume to add that I know enough about this required communication to be more than confident that those who read what George G. Hunter, III has written will be not only the better for it in their own attitude to the christian faith, but will find it a mine of practical information in their endeavor to share it with others.

Lord Donald Soper of Kingsway
Great Britain
April 1991

P R E F A C E

*H*ow do you communicate the christian faith to the growing numbers of "secular" people in the western world? Pastors and sunday school teachers who teach the faith week by week to professing Christians experience their assignment as increasingly difficult; so how do you communicate Christianity's meaning to people who do not darken church doors, who have no church background, who possess no traditional christian vocabulary, who do not know what we are talking about? The question presses us with greater intensity as we realize that the countries and populations of the western world have become "mission fields" once again.

I have been obsessed with this question for over 25 years. I experienced christian conversion and a call to the ministry as a senior in high school, in Miami, Florida. Soon I was absorbed in the Scriptures and enculturated into the Methodist Church, and even acquired a "ministerial tone" in near-record time. For the summer of 1962, while still in divinity school, I was assigned to do "unconventional evangelism" in a section of Santa Monica, California, known as "Muscle Beach." I spent the summer conversing with people in a "beatnik" coffee house, a "gay" bar, a house of prostitution, a pool hall, an "iron pumping" pavilion, and with drug addicts on the boardwalk and "surfers" on the beach. What an astonishing range of sub-cultures in one location! But they all shared one feature in common: they wondered what I was talking about! They were all secular. They lived their lives, many desperately, in terms of this world alone. My "churched" culture, with its jargon and rituals, robed choirs and stained glass, pews and pulpits, hymnals and handbells, was almost as alien to them as if it were imported from China or the Middle Ages or Venus.

My unconventional friends were not familiar with someone from the Church "invading" their turf! But about three dozen of them responded enough to help me begin with their questions and concerns. I used words they could understand, I shed the ministerial tone, and I learned to "speak like someone from this planet." Four of my new friends discovered faith that summer— not an impressive harvest for eight weeks of ministry. But the experience rubbed my face in questions about communicating the christian faith to secular people that I have struggled with ever since.

The next May, while browsing at the book store at my Methodist Annual Conference, I purchased Donald Soper's 1960 Lyman Beecher lectures at Yale Divinity School—*The Advocacy of the Gospel*. I (unofficially) excused myself from the conference's sessions that day, consumed Soper's lectures, and began making sense of my Muscle Beach experience. Soper, a British Methodist parson, had been interpreting the christian faith for thirty years from a soap box in London's open-air forums to a range of secular doubters and hecklers. The Yale lectures presented his insights from that longitudinal apostolic experiment.

Soper was the first "reflective practitioner" that I read who focused on the art of reaching secular people. Books like *The Secular City* by Harvey Cox and *Foolishness to the Greeks* by Lesslie Newbigin, helped us understand how the West was secularized and why it was once again a mission field, but you could read them and still not know what to *do*. The gap between theory and practice was a canyon. But Donald Soper worked at the practical challenge, in as demanding a setting as one could imagine, and learned from this "field experience" as well as from books.

While studying at Princeton Seminary, I read historians, philosophers, and sociologists on the development, shape, and challenge of secularity. I wrote a Ph.D. dissertation for Northwestern University on the British version of the problem. Over the years, I have interviewed hundreds of secular people and christian converts. I have also searched for other reflective

14

practitioners; I discovered a dozen who help inform this project. Here and there, some person or church is working at the apostolic task, and reflecting upon the experience, but no one has gathered and organized what is known about effective apostolic ministry to secular people in the West.

I have spoken on this topic at Billy Graham Schools of Evangelism, in courses at the Perkins School of Theology of Southern Methodist University, and at Asbury Theological Seminary, and for lectureships at Winebrenner Theological Seminary and Southern Nazarene University. In November 1989, I delivered four lectures on "Communicating Christianity to Secular People" for the annual Church Growth Lectureship at Fuller Theological Seminary's School of World Mission. Three reflective practitioners helped inform the project at that stage—Donald Soper, Robert Schuller, and Samuel Shoemaker.

Today Donald Soper continues his "soap box" advocacy to London's secular people in open-air meetings. His mission in these forums is pre-evangelistic and apologetic; that is, to advocate and explain the christian faith as a "redemptive approach to life as a whole," not merely the soul and family, as relevant good news which is intellectually worth considering. The meeting format is question and answer, challenge and response, with secular people (including "hecklers") voicing the questions and challenges. Soper responds to about 50 questions and challenges in a typical open-air meeting, which means he has fielded tens of thousands of questions and challenges. Lord Soper comments: "I do not pretend to know all of the answers to people's questions; but I do know all of the questions!" Soper may have a more extensive exposure to the minds of secular people than any other public Christian of the twentieth century. For years, he published a series of "Tower Hill" books that put people's questions in categories, in which he shared the answers that proved most helpful. Interviews with him generated additional insight about reaching secular people.

Robert Schuller, a clergyman for the Reformed Church of America in the USA, contrasts with Donald Soper in a thousand ways, but he shares the obsession to communicate meaningfully to secular people. Schuller began his Garden Grove Community Church (now the "Crystal Cathedral") as a *mission* to unchurched people. He planned the first services and programs of the church after extensive interviews with unchurched people in his ministry area. Each phase of the church's historic development and growth has been informed by "market research" data from the target unchurched population. His ministry now reaches millions through his "Hour of Power" television program and his "Possibility Thinking" books. He explains that "for 30 years my ministry has been a mission to unbelievers. I have seen my calling as communicating spiritual reality to secular people, people who aren't ready to believe in God. I have been trying to carry on a dialogue with persons who aren't ready to listen to God-talk." For years, Schuller and his staff have shared their discoveries in pastors' conferences at the Garden Grove church, and more recently in his book *Your Church Has a Fantastic Future.* Interviews with Schuller also produced invaluable insight.

The late Samuel Shoemaker was the leading evangelical minister of the Episcopal Church in the USA. He served pioneering pastorates in New York City and Pittsburgh, and he advanced the christian cause among unchurched people in those cities. He was the founder of Faith At Work and the spiritual father of Alcoholics Anonymous and its many spinoff programs. He identified the "Twelve Steps" by which any person, with group support, could discover the power of God and recover from any unmanageable problem. Shoemaker devoted his life to understanding and reaching people who do not know what Christians are talking about. He averaged two scheduled "interviews" per day with unchurched people for his entire career, and developed approaches to them that are perennially viable. Although I never knew or interviewed Shoemaker, he left his insights in the most extensive literature of any of my sources. His poem "I Stand By the Door" captures the vision of my entire project.

The late Donald McGavran encouraged me to expand the Fuller lectureship to book length by expanding my insights and by drawing from other reflective practitioners. He also sensed the existence of a scattered lore worth collecting. First, I added insights gained from the writings of, and interviews with, two more giants of progressive twentieth-century evangelicalism. Canon Bryan Green is a celebrated Anglican Evangelist who focuses on the evangelization of urban people. Green is the author of *The Practice of Evangelism*, is the rector emeritus of Birmingham, England, and was a widely read columnist. Sir Alan Walker is an Australian Methodist who served as superintendent of Sydney's Methodist Central Mission, and as director of evangelism for the World Methodist Council. He has preached and led training events in virtually every country of the western world and in every Communist nation except Albania and North Korea, and so he draws upon the widest experience of any of my sources.

Seven American communicators round out the roster. Donald Morgan's apostolic approach to secular people helped turn around one of New England's most historic Congregational churches. Jim Harnish planted and grew a pioneering United Methodist church to reach the Disney World population of Orlando. Bruce Larson led renewal movements to raise up an apostolic laity, then implemented his theories in the renaissance of University Presbyterian Church in Seattle before joining Schuller at the Crystal Cathedral. Kenneth Chafin served as director of evangelism for the Southern Baptist church and as dean of the Billy Graham Schools of Evangelism. He taught at two seminaries, pastored downtown city churches in Houston and Louisville, and he pioneers in ministries to people who aren't "churchbroke." In 1980 Rick Warren planted the Saddleback Valley Community Church in Orange County, California, to reach unchurched people. Today the church averages 4,500 in attendance and has planted 15 daughter congregations. In 1975 Bill Hybels launched a similar experiment to reach secular people in the northwest quadrant of metropolitan Chicago. Today the Willow Creek Community Church averages over 14,000 in attendance at weekend "seekers services," and grows at a rate of about 1,000 per year. In addition to interviewing Bill Hybels, reading his books, and auditing many of his tapes, I also interviewed Lee Strobel—a Willow Creek convert who often covers for Hybels in the pulpit and serves as the church's director of communications.

I thank all of these people for generously contributing to this project. Though my roster of reflective practitioners is interdenominational and international, I am embarrassed that they are all white, male, English-speaking clergy. Undoubtedly, other observers will learn from preachers like William Temple, E. Stanley Jones, J. Wallace Hamilton, Norman Vincent Peale, and Leslie Weatherhead; women like Eugenia Price, Dorothy Sayers, and Rebecca Pippert; laymen like G. K. Chesterton and C. S. Lewis; and leaders among ethnic populations, like Martin Luther King, Jr. (The history and challenge of each ethnic population is sufficiently distinct to warrant its own research project.) Furthermore, the gathering of modern apostolic lore will not approach completion until reflective practitioners and congregations have been studied in a dozen European languages.

I especially thank the colleagues who made suggestions from the earlier lectures—notably Win Arn, Eddie Gibbs, Peter Wagner, and Herb Miller. I also thank my colleagues at Asbury Theological Seminary's School of World Mission and Evangelism—Ron Crandall, Everett Hunt, Darrell Whiteman, Matt Zahniser, and Pat Richmond, for the contagious power of a shared vision.

This book attempts to draw together and systematize what is known about effective apostolic ministry to secular people in the West. The introduction summarizes the history of the "secularization process" that brought the christian movement to its new challenge in the countries of the western world. The first chapter presents a profile of the "secular people" that secularization has produced, and the second chapter features some of the known themes and strategies for reaching people who fit the profile. The third chapter is the "heaviest" chapter, but worth the trip! It unpacks communication principles and models that can help communicators and churches more effectively engage secular people. The fourth and fifth chapters profile the type of Christians and the type of churches that help searching secular people find their way into christian faith. Both profiles feature characteristics of Christians and churches that can be rehearsed and emulated; we and our churches can become more like them!

The following pages contain a mere fraction of what we will one day know about effective mission in the western world. But they contain enough insight from communicators, congregations, and converts to help 99 percent of our churches to triple the number of new Christians they help into faith and thereby become contagious movements in their communities.

How to
Reach
Secular
People

How the West Was Lost

*G*eoffrey lived five hundred years ago, in the market town of Beverly, in the Yorkshire region of northeast England. Geoffrey was a tall furniture craftsman, a sheep herder, a husband, and father of five girls and two boys. He loved to design furniture, and he felt close to the Creator when he was creating furniture. He loved to herd his sheep, which grazed in the common pasture outside the town. Tending his sheep kept Geoffrey in touch with the rhythms of nature and God's "natural revelation"; and Geoffrey cared for his sheep and knew their names, and thought often of the Good Shepherd who laid down his life for humanity.

"Times were changing" in this market town of two thousand people. The town's weavers were moving into the countryside beside streams—to harness water power. Many families were replacing the thatched roofs of their mud and timber houses with red tile—to reduce threat of fire. Cathedrals and parish churches were replacing frescoes with stained-glass windows.

In these changing times, Geoffrey heard rumors of corruption in the Church, that even Franciscans now lived in luxury. But, for Geoffrey, this was mere rumor. The priest at Beverly Minster loved the townspeople, and his devoted manner in baptisms, weddings, last rites, funerals, confessions, and the mass suggested the goodness of God. The priest was no great orator, but he was the only show in town; and he was wise to feature, one Sunday per month, a traveling Dominican friar who told mesmerizing stories from Scripture and church history. Beverly Minster, still an exquisite example of Gothic cathedral architecture, dominated Beverly's modest skyline and was the setting for the town's social life. The cathedral's many activities bathed people's minds in medieval christian images and ideas. Its ministry performed, and informed, each rite of passage in each person's life. It rehearsed the children in their catechism. The minster's stained-glass panorama of prophets, apostles, saints, and martyrs reminded the people of the Dominican's stories; indeed, as families visited the cathedral, parents told the stories to their children, as they would one day tell their children.

Geoffrey, like most of his peers five centuries ago, was illiterate, but his mind was immersed in Christianity. He knew, by heart, many sayings and teachings of Jesus, many doctrines of the church, and many stories from the Scriptures and christian tradition. G. M. Trevelyan, the social historian, tells us that "religion and the language of religion surrounded his life."[1] Furthermore, Geoffrey and his generation thought much about death, and feared it. His age had experienced epidemics, famines, plagues, and the Black Death; and Geoffrey had already lived beyond the average life span of 35. Moreover, Geoffrey's generation still lived with Ptolemy's map of the cosmos in their minds. Their universe was a three-layer structure—with an enchanted earth sandwiched between heaven and hell, the natural theater for the visits of angels and demons. Amidst it all, Geoffrey lived his life in earnest, and often talked seriously with his children about their lives and futures, and encouraged them to consider church vocations; in time, two daughters became nuns, and one son became an acclaimed Dominican storytelling preacher.

* * * * *

Today, 500 years and 20 generations later, a direct descendent of Geoffrey, named Sidney, lives in Phoenix, Arizona, a metropolis approaching two million people. Sidney, in several ways, resembles his ancestor. He too is tall. He appreciates animals and the outdoors. He appreciates exquisite furniture, and he manages a furniture store.

But Sid's identity, world, and life experience come from a different galaxy than Geoffrey's. Sid lives in a climate-controlled condominium, with cordless telephone, answering machine, microwave oven, home gym, personal computer with laser printer, and remote control cable TV with VCR. He lives alone, following a divorce, but often telephones his grown son and daughter. He plans to marry again, a resolve recently clarified with the discovery that his fiancé is pregnant.

Unlike Geoffrey, Sidney can read and is a college graduate. But he knows nothing of Geoffrey's depth and meaningful world of ideas.

Sidney's mind is anesthetized by the "junk food of the mind" served up by an endless diet of men's magazines, formula novels, game shows, situation comedies, soap operas, shallow movies, and synthetic friends. Sidney knows nothing about Christianity, apart from negative impressions of TV evangelists. He cannot name the four Gospels. He cannot recite, and would not recognize, the Lord's Prayer. He does not fear death. Indeed, he lives with the illusion that a premature death "couldn't happen" to him; consequently, his golfing buddy who peddles Prudential life insurance has not sold Sid "a piece of the rock." Sid does not think often of religion or the Church, but when he does, it is with vague suspicion, including the suspicion that clergy represent some third gender. Sid has no conscious christian background, memory, or vocabulary, though he is superstitious and will attribute an "off day" in golf to "bad luck." If you commended Christianity to Sid, you would not find him an atheist, saying, "I don't believe in your God," nor an agnostic, saying, "I don't know if I believe in your God"; because Sid is an Ignostic, saying, "I don't know what you are talking about." But he would add, "There must be some truth in religions; otherwise there wouldn't be so many of them."

* * * * *

Geoffrey was typical of his time, a period of a "Christian Society" in which most everyone in the Western world believed, belonged to the Church, and was scripted by its rites and teachings. Historians call that period "Christendom." Christendom began in the fourth century A.D., when the Church picked up the pieces of a fallen Roman Empire and, with a vision of God's purpose, "attempted to create a Christian civilization, to shape laws consonant with the biblical teaching, to place kings and emperors under the explicit obligation of Christian discipleship."[2] The Church defined the purposes for each area of life, so government, education, art, architecture, literature, music, personal morality, community life, and even economics marched to Christianity's drum. The Church became the source and center of Western Civilization, influencing every area of Western humanity's life, thought, and activity.

Sometimes the Church's influence bordered on monopoly. If people were educated, they got it from the Church. Art and music served christian themes. The Church even became a prominent land holding institution.[3] With variations, and periodic regional expansions, this arrangement by which the Church pervaded western culture lasted for nine or ten centuries. Within the arrangement, the Church shaped a cultural environment in which, presumably, all western people were "Christians."

But since that time, the West has been substantially lost, to the extent that Sidney is fairly typical of his age today. As measured by the simple indicator of church attendance, nations that were once substantially Christian are now largely lost to the christian movement. The percentage of people even attending church on an average Sunday has declined to 6 percent in West Germany and Italy, to between 1 and 3 percent in the Scandinavian countries, to 12 percent in Great Britain. In Canada, the percentage of people attending Church on an average Sunday is less than half what it was 40 years ago; in Australia, less than half what it was 25 years ago. Christianity's influence has substantially declined in the United States as well, a fact obscured by the United States' relatively constant church attendance (about 40 percent, in surveys), because much American church attendance is "Christo-pagan"; that is, American civil religion in christian clothing. Some churches concoct a hash from ingredients like patriotism, moralism, cultural values (like materialism and the quest for the perfect "high"), with some wisdom from "celebrities" mixed with selected Bible verses, and then they serve the hash as "Christianity"; that hash panders to people's tastes and inflates "church attendance" statistics, though the hash is far from real Christianity and leaves people's souls malnourished.

The Church's missionary challenge in the West today is thus complicated by the fact that most western populations have been exposed to some distorted or diluted expression of Christianity that inoculates people against the real thing, at least in its traditional forms. Alan Walker, who has preached and observed in 74 countries—including all the secular European countries and all the Communist countries except Albania and North Korea, concludes that "the Western world is now the toughest mission field on earth. There is now more resistance to the christian faith in the heart of old Christendom than anywhere else—England, Europe, Scandinavia, Canada, Australia, and New Zealand. Only in the United States is the church more than a minority movement."[4] Meanwhile, the christian movement has experienced great expansion in Africa, Asia, and

Latin America, and has demonstrated great tenacity, vitality, and growth in China, Russia, and most other Communist nations—even, and especially, during persecution. Remarkably, "more people go to church in Moscow than in London."[5]

HOW "SECULARIZATION" HAPPENED

How was the West lost? And how can the West be engaged by the gospel again? Those questions are important because the West is once again a vast mission field. In the United States alone, there are at least 120 million functionally undiscipled people (aged 14 or older). Ralph Winter announced in 1974 that the challenge of reaching the "Unreached Peoples" of the developing world would constitute the third and "final" era in the history of mission, but he presupposed a static world.[6] We now know that the western nations, who historically sent missionaries to the rest of the earth, are now mission fields themselves once again. They are arduous mission fields. Our challenge to reach the undiscipled populations of North America, Europe, and Australia will require as sophisticated a mission strategy as any mission field in the world today, or at any time in history. The whole world has a stake in Christianity's challenge to rewin the West because, as Harold Turner exclaimed during a lecture, "Western culture is now becoming the culture of all peoples, but it is increasingly sick—and the whole bit is being exported, including our social problems, to the whole world. And so we must solve this for the sake of the whole world."

The West was lost when the "Christendom" arrangement disintegrated. Geoffrey's world no longer exists; it is scarcely a memory. The cause of Christendom's disintegration was a massive "secularization" process within western history in the last five or six centuries, a process that continues today. An example of the secularization process occurred, repeatedly, over much of Europe in the fifteenth and sixteenth centuries, when the armies of various nobles and barons sacked the monasteries and seized church property; they said at the time that the property was being "secularized," that is, withdrawn from the control of the Church. We see from that example that "secularization" may be defined as "the withdrawal of

25

whole areas of life, thought, and activity from the control or influence of the Church.''[7] The Church experienced lost influence in every area of western society's life—from education to government, economics, art, architecture, literature, music, personal morality, and community life. Today no one even pretends that western culture still marches to Christianity's drum. The nearly complete secularization of the West is the Great New Fact confronting the entire western Church.

There are variations in the secularization process. The story of the secularization of economics varies from the story of literature's secularization, which varies from the secularization stories of government, and the arts, but the secularization of all areas of western life and thought share a common history involving *two fundamental causes* of western secularization.

SIX WATERSHED EVENTS

The first cause of Christendom's decline and the secularization of the West is located in a series of six major cultural events spanning several centuries. This discussion does not do them justice, but serves as a synopsis to remind us of the ''big picture.''

1. Secularization began with the *Renaissance*, an intellectual and cultural movement from the mid-fourteenth century to the early sixteenth century, led by Erasmus and Bacon. Essentially, the Renaissance represents the West's rediscovery of ancient Greek philosophy, science, and literature. The Renaissance affected western people in three ways. First, it redirected people's attention from God, another world, and theological matters to this world, to humans, and to humanity's progress. The ancient shibboleth of the Greek sophist Protagoras became the battlecry of the Renaissance: ''*Man* is the measure of all things.'' Second, the Church's worldview was, for centuries, the only comprehensive worldview available to Europeans. But the recovery of Greek philosophy gave people another option for understanding life and the world, thereby introducing pluralism and a new source of doubt to western minds. Third, the Renaissance created the cultural soil out of which humanism eventually emerged as a major and perennial competitor to christian truth claims and ethics.

26

2. The breakup of Christendom continued with the Protestant *Reformation*, led by Luther and Calvin. The Reformation removed Church influence from western life by dividing the Church and by turning the Church's attention away from the management of society and inward toward renewal, reorganization, and theological matters.[8] The Renaissance and the Reformation provided the one-two punch that got secularization rolling. During Luther's lifetime, the people said "Erasmus laid the egg, and Luther hatched it!"

3. Secularization continued with the rise of *Nationalism* and the rise of proud independent nations in what had once been a comparatively united Europe. The nationalistic spirit that swept Europe killed Christendom as a political entity and undercut the understanding of a common humanity that had largely prevailed in Christendom. Moreover, nationalism led to unprecedented warfare between the peoples of Europe—including the two world wars of this century. The experience of war induced disillusionment and doubts about the Church's God.

4. The rise of *Science* challenged Christendom's prescientific assumptions about the universe and human life. It would be difficult to exaggerate the impact of science, and what passed itself off as "science," upon western consciousness, but its impact can be potently suggested when one recalls the impact of these six thinkers: Copernicus, Galileo, Newton, Darwin, Marx, and Freud:

Copernicus and Galileo, by discovering the structure of the solar system, challenged the Church's traditional understanding of the cosmos. Ptolemy had placed the earth at the center of the universe, with the sun revolving around it. But Copernicus and Galileo demonstrated that the earth revolves around the sun, and the earth's rotation on an axis gives us our days and nights; the cosmology assumed from the New Testament through the Middle Ages was now ludicrous.

Newton's theory of gravity challenged the doctrine of Providence, as traditionally understood. Prior to Newton, people assumed that God's providential hand kept the moon, planets, and stars in place. Newton's *Principia* demonstrated, mathematically, that the universe's cohesion could be explained by his theory of gravity, and for many people God was edged out of the providence business. The long-term effect of the Newtonian revolution was even greater, as people came to see the universe as a self-enclosed system, or a "machine" that did not require "God" to explain or manage it.

Darwin's theory of evolution challenged the doctrine of the creation and the nature of humankind—as traditionally understood. Darwin's *Origin of Species*, with theories of natural selection, survival of the fittest, and progressive evolution, made it possible for people to understand their species in a very different way—as rational animals, without the dignity and purpose assumed in the biblical doctrine of creation.

Marx's writings provided an alternative to the traditional christian understanding of the goal of history. Marx seems to have retained the Judeo-christian structure of history, but he substituted for Christianity's promised Kingdom of God a promised economic utopia.

Freud wrote a question mark over religious belief and religious experience, charging that belief in God and experiences of God could be explained psychologically, and thereby explained away as an "illusion."[9]

5. The *Enlightenment* built upon the Renaissance to escalate the West's secularization. The Enlightenment is such a colossal cause of secularization that some writers, like Newbigin, treat it as virtually the only cause. The Enlightenment swaggered into European history with enormous confidence in human reason, and it left an intellectual legacy that has affected western society ever since. Enlightenment thinkers believed that human beings are intrinsically good and reasonable, but that their environment makes them less good and reasonable. Enlightenment leaders taught that beneath the world's diverse religions is a common "natural religion" universally present in human nature. Enlightenment leaders were confident that morality and society could be based on reason alone, without revelation or religion.[10] Enlightenment thinkers believed that science, technology, and education would deliver "inevitable progress." Some children of the Enlightenment saw the universe in terms of Newton's machine, assuming that the universe is self-contained and that the idea of God is therefore superfluous—not needed to understand the universe.[11] Furthermore, the Enlightenment trumpeted "human dignity" and "human rights" and inspired movements working for a more just and humane society, thereby providing a radical alternative to christian teachings and christian service. The Enlightenment thus encouraged doubt about Christianity and provided beliefs and causes that seemed to replace it, and ushered in "modernity."

6. If the Enlightenment escalated the secularization process, *Urbanization* stampeded it. Great Britain, in the eighteenth-century Industrial Revolution, became the world's first substantially urban country, but other European countries were not far behind. The

United States population has moved from 20 percent urban in 1870, to 40 percent in 1900, to 70 percent by 1980, and will approach 90 percent urban in 2000 A.D. Australia is no longer the "Outback" oriented nation featured in *Crocodile Dundee*; 85 percent of her people are urban, 70 percent live in the ten largest cities. Urbanization is the siamese twin of secularization. It has amplified the effects of secularization and has profoundly, if subtly, affected the God consciousness of urban secular populations. William Blake observed, in England's eighteenth-century Industrial Revolution, that "great things happen when men and mountains meet, but these things do not happen when men jostle in the street." Ralph Waldo Emerson, during the nineteenth-century Industrial Revolution in North America, is said to have confessed: "I look upon cities as great conspiracies; I always feel some loss of faith upon entering one."

HOW THE CHURCH ALIENATED THE PEOPLE

If the first cause of Christianity's loss of influence upon western people and culture was such a series of events—Renaissance, Reformation, Nationalism, Science, Enlightenment, and Urbanization,[12] the second cause was the Church's pathological pattern of responses to these events—responses that undermined the Church's credibility and distanced the people from her witness.

For instance, the Church conflicted early and persistently with Science. She tried to control what could (and could not) be researched, as in prohibiting Leonardo's study of cadavers to understand human anatomy. The Church tried to control what conclusions could (and could not) be reached or taught from scientific inquiry, as in banning Copernicus' books for 200 years, and in forcing Galileo to disown his discoveries in astronomy. The Church seems to have fought a reactionary war against Science at almost every opportunity, an unnecessary war! People like Newton and Galileo, and even Darwin, never understood themselves to be the enemies of the Church. But the Church's behavior made it appear to be the enemy of thought, rationality, and truth.

Protestant Churches became inordinately identified with the

nationalism sweeping Europe. Much of Protestant Christianity lost the vision of a common humanity and contributed to the chauvinism that separated nation from nation and led to many wars. Few people in the West had reason to associate Protestant Christianity with the Prince of Peace, and many observed this wing of the Church betraying him.

The Roman Catholic Church was strongest in the European countries where the Enlightenment was most vigorous, and widely opposed the Enlightenment's causes. Something happens to the Church's credibility every time she fails to throw her influence behind movements working for justice and democracy. Throughout Catholic Europe, the Church sided with monarchs and money, as later the Russian Orthodox Church did in Russia and Catholicism in Latin America. The effect, everywhere, has made the Church appear reactionary and against progress, democracy, justice, and the people.

Likewise, the western Church (especially Protestantism) has been paranoid of cities and reluctant to accept, or even perceive, urban challenges. Many people believe that the Church once had the West's urban working people but subsequently lost them; but in fact, it never had them, because the Church never reached out to city people with churches and clergy at all proportionate to the numbers of people in cities. Most denominations still distribute their churches and clergy as though we minister to territorial "parishes"— a model more consistent with the way the people previously were scattered in towns and across the countryside than the way they are stacked in cities today.

So Bertrand Russell wrote in his *History of Western Philosophy* (with some exaggeration) that "the churches, everywhere, opposed for as long as they could, practically every innovation that made for an increase of happiness and knowledge here on earth."[13] Many christian scholars are forced by the evidence to agree. David Edwards attributes secularization *chiefly* to the clergy's failure to transcend nationalism, to understand science and democracy, and to reach urban industrial workers. As a consequence of the secularizing events in Europe and the Church's counterproductive responses, Edwards observed eastern Europe as officially atheistic. In western Europe a small minority attend church, "skepticism is widespread, neither politics nor daily life is often profoundly influenced by the teaching of the churches," and "the average European has lost any vivid sense of God and any religiously based sense of right and wrong.'' Indeed, much of Europe experiences secularization as ''a process by which explicit religion becomes private, problematic, marginal and, in the end, eccentric.''[14]

SECULARITY IN DIFFERENT SHAPES

To put secularization in perspective, observe that this force in western culture has its limits. Secularization is not inexorable, nor irrevocable, and it is influenced and ''bent'' by other major forces in western history. Martin Marty has demonstrated, in *The Modern Schism: Three Paths to the Secular*, that the schism between the Church and western culture has taken at least three different forms.[15]

One form, characteristic of the European continent, is ''Utter Secularity.'' This form, typified by Voltaire and Marx, featured an open clash of doctrines involving ''a formal and unrelenting attack on gods and churches and a studied striving to replace them.'' In such a hostile secular environment, many people ''lost their faith.''

The second form, characteristic of Great Britain, is ''Mere Secularity.'' In this form, God and the churches are not attacked; they are ignored by people preoccupied with this world and their daily routines. Mere Secularity retains the shell of Christendom—a religious coronation of the monarch, a state Church, bishops in the House of Lords, religion taught in the schools, but without much meaning, power, or commitment. For most of the English, Christianity is equated with moral goodness, and most English people regard themselves as ''Christians''— in the sense that they are civilized and are not barbarians! Many people lose their faith in this ''mere'' secular environment too, though more incrementally and less consciously. Charles Darwin's own experience is representative: ''I gradually came to disbelieve in Christianity as a divine revelation. . . . This belief crept over me at a very slow rate, but was at last complete. The rate was so slow that I felt no distress, and have never since doubted for a single second that my conclusion was correct.''

The third form, characteristic of the United States, is ''Controlled

31

Secularity.'' The dominant religion in the United States is a folk religion which deifies traditional American values. This civil religion retains and uses the symbols of traditional Christianity, but with the meanings changed. So in the nineteenth century, christian symbols were used to support American imperialism as ''Manifest Destiny.'' In the twentieth century, Christianity is widely equated with the religiosity of *Readers Digest,* and some churches with large attendance reinforce this heretical equation, rather than liberate people from their cultural idolatry into biblical faith.

Although secularity takes different regional and cultural forms, Christianity in each form has lost most of its influence. A vast majority of the people in western culture are no longer christian disciples by anyone's serious definition. They live their lives, personal and public, not consciously influenced or shaped by Christianity. Christianity is no longer the dominant privileged religion of western nations. Indeed, western nations now ferment with many religious and philosophical options, and Christianity must now *compete* on its merits if it is to rewin the West.

Three other observations place secularity in perspective.

First, other religions and worldviews are also experiencing secularization and losing their earlier influence with large populations. Japanese culture's historic relation to Shinto has experienced substantial secularization since World War II. Most primal religions lose control of their people when they move to the cities. The phenomenon of Iran's Ayatollah Khomeini represents Shi'ite Islam's attempt to stand against the tide of secularization eroding Islamic cultures. Furthermore, we now observe, from China, to Russia, to the Soviet Union's satellite states and even Albania, the secularization of Communism's influence upon its peoples. Each experience of secularization is distinct, but common features include the impact of science, nationalism, humanism, urbanization, and the *de facto* westernization of much of the earth. Given the sudden collapse of the Communist parties, much of what we are learning about communicating Christianity to secular western pagans can inform our mission to populations in cultures now removed from the former influence of other religions and worldviews.

Second, though ''secularity'' is not synonymous with the ideology of ''secularism,'' the secularized soil out of any religion breeds

32

"secular*ism.*" Os Guinness observed, in an unpublished speech at Lausanne II in Manila, that

since 1900, the percentage of the world's atheistic and non-religious peoples (agnostics, secularists, communists and so on) has grown from 0.2 percent to 21.3 percent—in other words from less than one-fifth of one percent to over one fifth of the world's population. This is the most dramatic change on the entire religious map of the twentieth century. Secularists, or people with no religious commitment, now form the second largest bloc in the world, second only to Christians and catching up fast (at the rate of 8.5 mission 'converts' a year).

Third, it is also noteworthy that Christianity is not alone in experiencing difficulty in communicating its message and way of life in a secularized culture. Virtually every religion, philosophy, and ideology finds that secularity has not made its way easy, but a secular culture especially challenges religions like Christianity whose core truth claims are not negotiable.

SECULARIZATION APPRAISED

Upon reflection, how should the christian movement appraise the loss of Christendom and the rise of a secular culture? Dozens of scholars and leaders have given much thought to this; the following lines of thought are representative.

R. H. Tawney, in *Religion and the Rise of Capitalism*, claimed that the loss of Christendom was a genuine loss for western humanity.[16] Christendom, for all its flaws, was a considered attempt at a christian society, and it achieved an impressive level of human community, economic justice, and peace. He lamented that, following Christendom's decline, the Church narrowed the sphere of her thought and interests to individualistic and "spiritual" matters, and lost her own social philosophy, and is now prey to whatever social philosophy is fashionable.

But, a century before Tawney, Søren Kierkegaard mounted an *Attack Upon Christendom*, celebrating Christendom's decline, because "when everybody is a Christian, nobody is a Christian."[17] Kierkegaard saw that when one understands oneself to be a Christian because one is born in a so-called christian country, has been baptized and scripted with a few christian values, one is only "playing Christianity . . . like soldiers play war on the parade grounds," and this "illusion" almost prohibits anyone from becoming a Christian in the New Testament sense of following Jesus Christ and conforming one's life to God's will. Kierkegaard yearned for the day when the only "Christians" would be real followers of Jesus Christ.

Rudolf Bultmann's essay "The New Testament and Mythology" reminded us that western populations now live after the Copernican revolution in cosmology, and so "we no longer believe in the three-storied universe which the creeds take for granted."[18] We are called, therefore, to meaningfully reinterpret the New Testament's message to our own time and culture.

Dietrich Bonhoeffer, building upon Kierkegaard and claiming that Bultmann "did not go far enough," saw some matters deeply from his prison cell.[19] In the advanced secularization he observed, Bonhoeffer concluded that most people now refer to "God," even "religious" people, as a "stop-gap god," or a *deus ex machina*. People characteristically refer to "god" as the cause of something they cannot explain, such as lightning, or they turn to "god" for help when they cannot otherwise help themselves, such as in sickness. He observed that, as people have to use "god" as an explanation less and less and have to call on "god" for help less and less, this "god is being edged out of the world," to the periphery of people's conscious world. But Bonhoeffer proclaimed that this creeping event in western consciousness is to be celebrated, because the *deus ex machina* is not the God of the Bible anyway; the biblical "God is the 'beyond' in the midst of our lives." Bonhoeffer welcomed secularization because it is "a clearing of the decks for the God of the Bible." He believed that a viable communicating form of Christianity in the future would assume a form of "religionless Christianity." Effective communication would avoid "religious jargon," and would "speak . . . in secular fashion of God." A faithful church in a post-christian era would commend the gospel and explain "the cost of discipleship," and would appeal to people in their strength, not just in their weakness.

More recently, Lesslie Newbigin's *Foolishness to the Greeks* sees that secular western people now live in terms of two worlds: (1) a Public World of "facts"—demonstrable by science, the same for everyone, to which all reasonable people agree, and (2) a Private

World of values and religious beliefs in which pluralism reigns and each person believes in something (or nothing) by choice.[20] Newbigin sees two special problems with this private world of beliefs and values: (1) The culture now assumes, as percolated down from the Enlightenment, that the essence of Christianity is the same as that of the other world religions, and that the different religions make up a mosaic from which people pick and choose. (2) Newbigin charges, agreeing with Tawney, that Protestant Christianity has largely accepted the public-private dichotomy and has withdrawn into the private sector, thereby securing a continuing place for itself but abdicating the central biblical convictions that "the earth is the Lord's and the fullness thereof" and that "Jesus is Lord" and "the light of the world."

OUR NEW "APOSTOLIC AGE"

Scholarly appraisals accepted, the Church in the western world needs to experience the paradigm shift that allows it to perceive the new missionary challenge in the secular West today. Indeed, the situation we face is much like what the early apostolic Church faced. What does this mean?

For the christian movement's first three centuries, the communication of Christianity had to achieve four objectives: (1) Facing a population with no knowledge of the gospel, the christian movement had to *inform* people of the story of Jesus, the good news, its claims, and its offer. (2) Facing hostile populations and the persecution of the state, the Church had to "win friends and *influence* people" to a positive attitude toward the movement. (3) Facing an Empire with several entrenched religions, the Christians had to *convince* people of Christianity's truth, or at least its plausibility. (4) Since entry into the faith is by an act of the will, Christians had to *invite* people to adopt this faith and join the messianic community and follow Jesus as Lord. These were the components of persuasion in the ancient apostolic setting.

The early Church was intentional about achieving each of these four objectives. They informed people by creatively communicating and interpreting their gospel in conversations, synagogue presentations, and open-air speaking. They influenced people's attitudes by their changed lives, their ministries of service, their love for one another, and by their love for nonchristians and even their enemies, even in martyrdom. They convinced people by reasoning from the Scriptures and by their common-sense apologetics. They invited responsive people to confess faith and be baptized into the messianic community.

Much later, when Christendom was in place, with the parish church at the center of community life and the Church informing every area of the culture's life, the informing, influencing, and convincing goals were achieved in people's enculturation. Most people were already informed in the faith's basics, were favorably disposed toward the faith, and already assumed its truth. So the christian communicator could largely focus on inviting people, who were already informed, convinced, and favorably inclined, to adopt the faith.

With the events of secularization and the Church's defensive reaction to those events, increasing numbers of people experienced alienation and a negative attitude toward the Church, withdrew from the churches, and in time many western people no longer understood, or recalled, the faith of their ancestors. Today, this secularization is so advanced in all of the countries of Europe, North America, and Australia that no communicator today has the luxury of beginning at point four and appealing for a response, because, as Donald Soper has observed, "Not one in every ten people has the remotest idea of what you and I within the church mean by 'religion.' "[21]

So the Church must begin farther back with people today. For centuries the Church was harvesting grain in fields already plowed, seeded and watered. But today we must first plow, seed, and water the fields before we can reasonably expect to gather harvests. For centuries, in basketball jargon, the Church always had "home court advantage," but today we occasionally play on a neutral court and usually on the opponent's court—if we play at all. Unfortunately, most churches still sit back and wait for people to come play on our court. But, as Donald Soper contends, most evangelism today presupposes that the Middle Ages are still with us, "and takes little or no account of the fact that the Church today is back in apostolic times."[22]

36

THE CHRISTIAN MOVEMENT'S EMERGING OPPORTUNITY

Coincidentally (or providentially), the Church's new apostolic challenge is joined by a rising opportunity more vast than anything the Church dared pray for. Today, Sidney's numbers are so legion that the secularization of the West has placed the Church in a missionary role here "at home," because most of our neighbors do not share our faith, or a memory of our faith, or our assumptions, or our vocabulary. The West is, once again, a vast mission field.[23] Until recently, however, the western Church has still behaved as though Christendom were still intact, as though a church's only role is to shepherd christian people in a settled christian society. But Newbigin's *Foolishness to the Greeks* has alerted many church leaders to the missionary challenge in Europe and North America, and, more recently, Diogenes Allen's *Christian Belief in a Postmodern World* suggests that Christianity's mission to the West now approaches an unprecedented opportunity.

Diogenes Allen argues that, due to twentieth-century revolutions in science and philosophy, the Enlightenment is now a spent force, and the period of "Modernity" it produced is spent too.[24] "Modernity" is essentially finished because most of the Enlightenment's key ideas have now been abandoned by leading scientists and philosophers, and by historical experience. We can now demonstrate, from a wide range of literatures, some significant changes.

1. Human beings are not as good and reasonable as enlightenment ideology taught; "There is an increasing recognition that evil is real and that it cannot be removed merely by education and social reform" (Allen, p. 5). Good legislation for, say, urban renewal, is aborted without good people to manage the programs. The corollary enlightenment view that knowledge is inherently good is also crumbling. The atomic age has demonstrated that knowledge can be made to serve good purposes *or* evil purposes, depending on the morality of the people controlling it.

2. Enlightenment teachings about a common "natural religion" in human nature have not survived examination (Allen, p. 185). There is no apparent common base that all the religions hold in common; indeed, their core worldviews contradict one another. For instance, the Jewish, Moslem, and Christian religions are theistic, Buddhism and Communism are atheistic, Hinduism and most primal religions are polytheistic. The eastern religions,

generally, are world renouncing; the western religions, generally, are world affirming.[25] The first argument for the "uniqueness" of Christianity is that each of the major religious traditions is unique! Far from sharing a common core, the religions appear most alike at the surface (for instance, all, or most, religions feature prayer or meditation), and more disimilar the deeper you go in each.

3. Society has proven incapable of developing, by reason alone, a consensus morality. The quest for "rational laws" for human behavior has been frustrated because, apparently, there are no such laws. Nor are there objective values upon which a consensus morality could be based; values are now seen to be culturally scripted, or a matter of preference. This represents a mammoth breakdown in the western tradition, because it programs the culture for moral anarchy and demonstrates no reason to support the long-held conviction that every person has intrinsic value.

4. Science and education have not liberated humanity from entrenched problems like crime, pollution, poverty, racism, and war, and this failure has crippled the notion of "inevitable" progress. A greater realism has replaced the earlier pollyanna optimism of the Enlightenment. We may be able to overcome these difficulties, but humanity's liberation from social bondage and nature's bondage is not assured, and certainly not "inevitable."

5. As twentieth-century scientists probed the mystery of the atom, the Newtonian view of the universe as a machine was not confirmed; indeed, nature at its core now appears random and mysterious. Consequently, many leading scientists and philosophers now admit the limits and fallibility of science, and the myth of complete "scientific objectivity." Many scientists and philosophers are no longer closed to the possibility of God—as the enlightenment script required, but now pursue it as an open and important question. Increasingly, sensible people want to know whether the universe is ultimate or not, why this universe exists rather than some other, and why this universe exists at all. They know that God is one possible answer to these questions.

This means that the pillars of "modern" western civilization, erected during the Enlightenment, are now crumbling. Allen observes that we are now in a period of culture lag—in which most people in the western world are not yet as aware as scientists and philosophers that the Enlightenment is over. But, Allen predicts, "when the dust settles," we will see that "the fields are ripe for the harvest."

The dust may be settling already. I attended an awards assembly at my daughter's middle school in Jessamine County, Kentucky. The new superintendent of schools, Dr. Lois Adams, addressed the student body. She encouraged each student to make every day count, to accept responsibility for themselves, and to believe they are "special." She delivered the "you are special" part of her address sensitively and effectively, but, as I studied several dozen faces, I could tell they were not buying it! They were afflicted with "MEGO"—an acronym for "my eyes glaze over!" The affirmation of every person's uniqueness and dignity was washing past them!

I think I know why. The youth are the products of too many losing experiences and negative messages to believe, easily, that they are special. Besides, you need *reasons* to believe in your own uniqueness and dignity. Historically, most people in the West have been able to believe in their dignity because they (a) were culturally "scripted" with biblical assumptions about human creation in "the image of God" or, more recently, (b) because they were scripted by enlightenment ideals. But the rising generation's glazed eyes, volatile feelings, and vulnerability to drugs tell us they are the first generation for whom the once powerful Enlightenment is now extinct. If we lift up our eyes, we may see that the western fields are already becoming "white unto harvest."

Profiling
the Secular Population

*T*he secularization process, by which the Church lost the central place and influence it enjoyed in the centuries of "Christendom," has produced a vast mission field in the western world. In today's secular West, the Church no longer enjoys a "home court advantage." The Church now faces the challenge of reevangelizing Europe and North America. We observe, in the United States alone, at least 120,000,000 secular people (14 or older). What do we really know about them?

To begin with the obvious, they are not a single homogeneous group; a secular population is composed of many distinct audiences—based on differences in ethnicity, culture, age, needs, education, socioeconomic class, etc. Russell Hale's interviews with unchurched people in the United States surfaced ten distinct types of unchurched people—seven of whom are substantially secular.[1]

Secular people vary in their consciousness of Christianity. Perhaps a third of them, like Sidney, have no christian memory; they are "ignostics"—that is, they don't know what Christians are talking about. Another third have a distant christian memory—they could identify Moses; they are "notional" Christians—who think of themselves as more or less Christian because they assume their culture is more or less Christian. Another third are "nominal" Christians—who are somewhat active in churches, but their religion is civil religion (which they mistake for Christianity) and most gospel washes past them. But all three subgroups are secular, for their lives are not significantly influenced by the christian faith. Their assumptions, vocabularies, decision making, and life-styles reflect no christian agenda. Furthermore, many persons in the first two groups are not "churchbroke"—that is, they don't know how to act in

41

church. So visiting a church can be a clumsy, even alienating, experience for them. The nominal Christians are churchbroke, and they know enough of the jargon and routine to pass themselves off as disciples, but they are driven by their own will and their culture's values.

THREE MYTHS ABOUT SECULAR PEOPLE

But beyond such obvious generalizations, how have five centuries of secularization changed people? What can be known about secular people that can inform more effective christian witness? What are the available points of contact with them, and available strategies for reaching them? Let's begin with three widely held beliefs about secular people that are not true.

First, some pundits have declared that secularization has erased all religious consciousness from people's minds, that there is no more religious *a priori* within human personality, and we are entering an age of "no religion." Not so. Western culture, as Ken Chafin observes, is much like ancient Athens where, in Acts 17, Paul reasoned with people influenced by a range of religions and philosophies—from Epicureanism and Stoicism, to various Gnostic and Mystery religions, to the cult of the Emperor.[2] Versions of these religions are around today, plus a range of others from astrology to Zen, while new religions continue to surface. In the early 1970s a 17-year-old Maharishi Guru filled Houston's Astrodome—dramatizing a religious movement that seemed, at the time, to be the wave of the future. The late 1980s saw the "New Age" movement on the crest of a wave. Other forms of religion have included the deification of the state—as in Nazi Germany; the deification of political ideologies—as in Communism; and the deification of specific cultures—as in Japanese Shinto or "the American Way of Life." Secularization has not made people less "religious." There is extensive evidence that people are incurably "religious," though some people feast, serially, from a growing menu of religious options that the Church no longer controls. Other people reflect the profile in Reginald Bibby's *Fragmented Gods.*[3] They report in church preference surveys the same religious affiliation as did their parents, and they participate in the traditional rites of passage, but they attend Sunday services less often and, like consumers, they "pick and choose religious fragments at will."[4] A belief here and a practice there. "Religion à la carte!"

Second, some gurus warn that secularization has erased moral consciousness, so that secular people are simply "immoral." But, in fact, secular people participate in many moral struggles and make an unprecedented number of moral choices. But, no longer "programmed" by christian enculturation, they receive the premises for moral choices more likely from parents, peers, or pop culture than from the Church or its Scriptures. Indeed, the twentieth century has seen an explosion of moral causes—from civil rights, human rights, women's rights, and animal rights, to pro-life and pro-choice, to anti-nuclear and anti-apartheid crusades, to humanitarian movements for refugees, famine victims, prisoners of conscience, and endangered species. As Harold Turner reminded us during an Asbury lecture, "Even the terrorist is driven by a moral passion."[5]

Third, some church leaders have a university professor friend who "lost his faith," and these leaders now imagine that all secular people are philosophically sophisticated geniuses who have read christian literature from Augustine to Zwingli and rejected the christian case *in toto* on rational grounds. But the vast majority of secular people are not epistemologically sophisticated; most are naive, superficial, gullible people who may fall for anything. Many are preyed upon by cults and authoritarian leaders; they buy anything promoted by their favorite "celebrity." Many of their thoughts are mere "tapes" out of their cultural scripting, such as "Too many hypocrites in the church." Our western mission field is filled with people who watch soap operas and believe that life mirrors the tube! A majority of secular people are not strongly literate. But most of them have a religious agenda, and they ask important religious questions (though not in traditional religious terms).

TEN CHARACTERISTICS OF SECULAR PEOPLE

Secular people are not, by and large, a-religious, immoral, or sophisticated. But what is true about them that christian communicators need to know? In what ways has secularization changed people that require us to change our assumptions and strategies? These are not new questions. A concerned faction within the Church has been struggling with these questions for much of this century, though usually at an abstract level. One such book, Lesslie Newbigin's *Foolishness to the Greeks*, has performed the service of awakening, in a broader range of church leaders, some interest in the christian mission to western societies.[6] But questions like this are most usefully answered from field data, including data from communicators already engaged in the new mission to the West, and in reflecting upon that engagement.

This chapter draws substantially from the lifetime insights of several "reflective practitioners" of communication to secular people who were introduced in the preface.[7] The reflections of these practitioners help us to identify ten characteristics of secular people that all christian communicators need to know. In each characteristic, I feature the insights of these reflective communicators which are confirmed by my own interviews with secular people and new Christians.

1. Secular people are essentially ignorant of basic Christianity

Donald Soper discovered, in his open-air forums, that most secular people are essentially ignorant about basic christian matters. In Christendom, Geoffrey and his peers, though illiterate, had an extensive working knowledge of Christianity. They knew many teachings of Jesus, many stories from Scripture and tradition, and many doctrines of the Church. Today, most "educated" people, like Sidney, are uninformed of basic Christianity. Many are biblically illiterate; they may not know the difference between the Old Testament and the New Testament, may not recognize the Lord's Prayer or a literary allusion to the prodigal son. Indeed, many secular people are misinformed about essential Christianity. Once they have been exposed to a distorted, diluted form of Christianity, they are inoculated against the real thing (or at least its traditional cultural forms)!

The secularization of consciousness, in many western cultures and subcultures, has now prevailed for three or four generations, which compounds the problem. Alan Walker explains:

> So today there is almost a complete ignorance of what the Christian gospel really is. You see, Christian knowledge and awareness are now the echo of an echo of an echo—too faint to be heard. This means, for example, a feeling of awkwardness, even embarrassment, at entering a sacred building. There is ignorance in the ways of Christian worship. Therefore such people no longer desire to enter churches. It means an almost complete ignorance of Christian stories, biblical references, the traditional language of the pulpit.[8]

Nor are secular people necessarily in a position to appropriate the full gospel once they are exposed to it, because, as Samuel Shoemaker stressed, in our consumer-oriented society, people approach religion as consumers, and they "buy" if it promises to meet their needs and wants. Most secular people are unacquainted with the basic assumption of the Bible—that God is their rightful Lord to whom they are accountable, who calls them to commit their lives to the will of God. They have no background for responding to Mother Teresa's challenge to "put yourself completely under the influence of Jesus." So, for several reasons, we can observe with Soper that secularization has "produced a situation in which those to whom we preach are not in any suitable condition to receive what we have to say."[9]

2. Secular people are seeking life before death

Donald Soper also discovered that, in contrast to the "death orientation" that characterized western populations until fairly recent times, most secular people today are "life oriented." In the long history before medicine's modern advances, western humanity's history was dominated by famines, epidemics, and plagues. Until recent times, sickness often brought death, corpses and funerals were commonplace, many people were obsessed with death, and strived for life after death. Today, most sicknesses are not crises but inconveniences, human life expectancy has more than doubled, and some people even deny their mortality.

Many secular people are aware of their mortality, but most of them fear extinction more than they fear hell or seek heaven. As Ken Chafin observes, "They wonder about 'when I am not.' The thought of themselves as no longer existing is the frightening thought." Consequently, they generally do not ask about life after death so much as they ask about real life this side of death. While seeking to salvage this life, they struggle to make sense of their life, to find meaning and purpose, to attain significance, and to make a contribution while they live.

Alan Walker believes that this shift in secular human consciousness is of such Copernican magnitude for the strategic church that the very motive for evangelism must now change. Once, when the population feared death and hell, the appeal of life after death, understandably, motivated the christian mission. "Religion used to be related to the moment of dying; now it must be related to the moment of living." Now we know that "to go on living apart from an acceptance of the love of God is the real tragedy."[10]

3. Secular people are conscious of doubt more than guilt

Donald Soper would coach the christian advocate to face one stark reality—that doubt is now the number-one factor in the secular audience. In Christendom, and until fairly recent times, guilt was the prominent feature of a nonchristian audience; people were conscious of personal guilt, for which they felt responsible and sought forgiveness. Today, many people still acknowledge that "guilt" is behind society's problems, but someone else's guilt—the "system," the establishment, their parent's generation, the younger generation, the communists, or the Arabs. People who feel guilty are more likely to go to a therapist for freedom from the feeling than to a priest for absolution. Soper observes that "the profound sense of personal guilt has almost disappeared."[11]

Soper quotes a predecessor, Dr. J. Ernest Rattenbury, who observed that, in the late nineteenth century, "you could count on a general sense of guilt. Now [by the 1930s] the only thing you can count on is a general sense of doubt."[12] There are several causes of this "age of dubiety," including the plural truth claims confronting people, the extensive spread of enlightenment ideas, the low credibility of the institutional church, and various cultural and peer group influences. In any case, "we have to speak . . . to hearers who are in various stages of doubt."[13] For the communicator, this means that

before we can make any impression upon those to whom we seek to preach today, we have to recognize that they are already in a resistant frame of mind. They have been encouraged to think very largely in terms of doubt, and the more authoritatively we claim to speak, the more likely we are to produce an ambivalent, if not a contrary, effect to that which we desire. This is the outstanding characteristic of the hearer.[14]

Soper concludes that, with secularization, "doubt has taken the place of guilt as the common factor in the constitution of the preacher's crowd."[15]

4. Secular people have a negative image of the Church

If many secular people have doubts about Christianity's truth claims, they also have a negative image of the Church. Specifically, they doubt the intelligence, relevance, and credibility of the Church and its advocates.

They doubt the Church's intelligence, or its capacity to know the Truth about ultimate matters, because they still place more confidence in science and common sense than in religion, and because they recall (however vaguely) that the Church has been proven wrong on many matters, and nothing has happened since to restore their confidence in the Church's "mind."

The people's doubts about the Church's relevance began when the Church reacted defensively to the events of secularization. The problem was amplified when, as Newbigin observes, our enlightenment culture divided life into a "public world" of facts—upon which everyone agrees, and a "private world" of values, beliefs, and religion—in which pluralism reigns and each person believes in something (or nothing) by choice. With the culture's decreasing need for a *deus ex machina* for help or explanation, and with the culture's perception of Christianity as relevant only to the private world of soul and family, more and more secular people feel no conscious need for what they see Christianity offering.

The secular charge that Christianity is "irrelevant" is not only rooted in history and the enlightenment worldview of western culture, but also in personal experience. Many secular people once experienced an apparently irrelevant church and generalized to all churches from that experience. Ken Chafin observes that, while many secular people have little christian memory, many have had—and remember—experiences in a church. Chafin reports that

many of these people drifted out of church because it didn't seem to make any difference. They drifted out as teenagers, as a part of their adolescent rebellion. Some of them grew up in irrelevant churches, or under irrelevant preaching. Most of them are not angry; they are indifferent to the Church. A yawning indifference is the big challenge that secularity presents to the Church. They do not think of Church as plugged into life where they are.

And most people don't differentiate between their feelings about Church and about God. They figure the Church represents God, so God must be sort of like the Church. So, if the Church is judgmental about their divorce, God must be.

Because secular people assume that the christian faith applies only to a private world of the soul and the family, they no longer perceive that "the hopes and fears of all their years" are met in Jesus Christ. The more extreme secularists may even view christian belief as "madness" or "insanity." In one of Donald Soper's open-air meetings, a heckler challenged Soper's sanity, saying, "If you are not mad, prove it." Soper, disconcerted by this unusual attack, played for time by asking the heckler to prove *he* was not mad; the man produced from his pocket a discharge certificate from a mental hospital! Soper, upon reflection, sympathized with the heckler.

What, in more technical language, is insanity? It is, surely, a condition in which what is going on in one's head is insulated from, or contrary to, what is going on all around it. If I live in a private world of my own which has nothing to do with the real world outside, I am mad. Insanity is disassociation and, in this sense, the heckler was, in his own intransigent way, calling attention to a very real problem for the Christian advocate.

Can it not be argued that Christianity, and more particularly the Church, is an example of irrelevance bearing no genuine relationship to the world of actual experience?[16]

As a tradeoff, Soper saw that while people have less felt need for what they perceive Christianity offering, they are increasingly *curious* about Christianity and Christians, and especially the credibility of Christians. They want to know what Christians believe, and whether believing makes any difference in their lives, and whether enough people believing it would make any practical difference in the world.

Writing from experience with secular people in Germany, Helmut Thielicke saw how supremely important is the Church's credibility with secular people. In *The Trouble with the Church* Thielicke observed several credibility gaps in western societies.[17] People, rightly, question the credibility of politicians making campaign promises and athletes advertising soft drinks. People, likewise, ask questions about the credibility of the Church and its advocates. They do not ask whether we in fact drink the soft drink we commend to others—they assume we probably do. "The question is rather whether [we] quench [our] own thirst with the Bible." Does believing it make any difference in our lives? Or are preachers just paid propagandists for the institutional church? Thielicke believed that the perceived "credibility of the witnesser" is the crucial variable in communicating Christianity in secular Europe today.

5. *Secular people have multiple alienations*

Virtually all effective gospel advocates become acutely aware of a fifth change in people from secularization and modernization—a deep and pervasive alienation.[18] In Christendom, it seems that people were secure and felt included, and their need "to belong" was essentially met through their work, extended family, and village life. But today, it is possible to describe many secular people in terms of multiple alienations. Many people are alienated from nature, as evidenced by sport killing, strip mining, endangered species, and the mounting ecological crisis. Many people are alienated from their neighbors, as evidenced by the anonymity of high-rise apartment dwellers and people's abuse of each other in economic transactions. Many people are alienated from the political and economic systems upon which their lives depend, as evidenced by the breakdown of lifetime job security and the bumper sticker reading "Don't vote for anybody. It only encourages them!'' Many people are alienated from their vocations, as evidenced by their expressed lack of meaning in their life work and their obsession with leisure pursuits.

Bruce Larson, in a private interview, adds the perception that alienated people are characteristically lonely. Larson observes that ''many people are dying of loneliness,'' that some medical professionals claim that loneliness is the number-one killer in America. So Larson asks people, ''If your child was dying or your spouse was divorcing you, who could you call at 2:00 A.M. and say 'I'm dying in a pile'? Who would be glad to hear from you? If you haven't got somebody, you're in bad shape.''

6. Secular people are untrusting

Robert Schuller reports that many secular people are untrusting. Schuller previously assumed, as did most theologians, that infants come into the world trusting, and then learn to distrust. But, from Eric Erikson's writings, he saw that the infant's clinging to the mother's breast ''is a demonstration of a lack of trust and inborn insecurity.''[19] The essence of sin, he believes, is lack of trust. People enter the world with this affliction, needing strokes, love, and affirmation from the earliest days. The problem is compounded by many experiences in our alienated society, in which people are burned, manipulated, and exploited so many times that their guard is up. Schuller believes that it is more useful to *relate* to a nonchristian ''as a nontrusting person—fearful and suspicious—than to relate to him or her as an 'evil' or 'depraved' or 'shameful' soul.'' He believes that ''God longs to release every person's human potential from the imprisoning, self-destructive fear and guilt that inhibit positive believing.''

Schuller also observes that the model of God in many secular minds reinforces their insecurity. Some people image God as the ''Grim Reaper'' who threatens people's lives, or the Santa Claus who gives presents based upon our goodness, or the Cop who watches for us to do something wrong, or the Duplicitous Politician who uses people and manipulates nations.[20]

7. Secular people have low self-esteem

Robert Schuller also observes that many secular people are afflicted with a loss of dignity, or low self-esteem. This fact is somewhat surprising. Dietrich Bonhoeffer, from his prison cell, expected increasing secularity to produce "strong" people, that is, "man come of age," so that the church would have to learn to speak more to people in their strength, no longer just in their weakness. There are individuals like that, but no one could have predicted the vast number of people today who do not believe in themselves, or affirm their identity, or positively value themselves, or feel a sense of self-worth.

Schuller is aware that various psychologists have identified some other need as the essential need of human personality.[21] Freud saw the desire for pleasure as basic, Adler saw power needs as fundamental, and Frankl identified humanity's widespread quest for meaning. Schuller respects all those views, especially Frankl's, but he believes that loss of dignity and low self-esteem are so epidemic that this could be the focus of the next reformation. He observes:

Our natural inability to trust God's love or to trust Christ's offer of salvation and forgiveness stems from our deep lack of self-worth. We simply do not value ourselves enough to believe that we can truly be loved unconditionally and nonjudgementally. So we resist at a profoundly deep level the divine invitation to salvation "by grace." Our innate sense of shame and unworthiness compel us to believe that we have to "earn love" and "do something."[22]

Schuller believes that self-esteem is the key to several struggles in secular people. He believes that a person's emotional fulfillment cannot be realized apart from a certain level of positive self-esteem, that people without a practicing faith will resort to materialism to compensate for the spiritual and emotional vacuum in their lives, and that appropriate positive self-esteem is finally realized only in covenantal relationships with God and the people of God. Relationships are crucial in self-understanding and self-worth because "I'm not what I think I am; I'm not what you think I am; I am what I think you think I am." Schuller proclaims the possibility of a "self-image transplant," and he challenges people to "go for it."[23]

Bruce Larson, now Schuller's Crystal Cathedral colleague, understands secular people as sinners—in the basic sense of estrangement, or life without God, and this estrangement afflicts them with three problems related to the self. (1) Secular people are self-centered. As babies, they come into the world screaming for food, for changing, for love. With growth, they cease screaming and learn to "work" their parents, their peers, and then their company for what they want, but they are still self-centered. (2) Secular people are self-deceived. Larson believes that "every family is dysfunctional," including every family in the Bible, so "we all come out of dysfunctional families"—not really knowing who we are. We come into the world as the "adored" kid like Joseph, or the "abhorred" kid like Jacob, or an "ignored" kid like Joseph's brothers. (3) This self-deception affects our self-esteem, so that every person "graduates" from the family with self-esteem that is either too low or too high, and without a clear and accurate identity.

8. Secular people experience forces in history as "out of control"

Ken Chafin observes that many secular people face the future with great anxiety, because they perceive history as "out of control." They experience history as an endless series of large-scale surprises, shocks, and threats—from the assassinations of John and Robert Kennedy and Martin Luther King, Jr., from the Vietnam war to the cold war to the sudden dismantling of the Soviet Union to the sudden Persian Gulf crisis, from volatile stock markets and oil prices to threats of recessions, unemployment, urban violence, the onslaught of drugs and the AIDS epidemic. Many people feel that "no one is in charge."

9. Secular people experience forces in personality as "out of control"

While many people experience forces in history as "out of control," many people also experience forces in their own personalities and families they cannot control. Samuel Shoemaker anticipated, in the 1940s and 1950s, the widespread self-destructive addictions that afflict many children of secular modernity. He worked extensively with alcoholics and saw their behavior patterns in people with other problems.[24] Contrary to Bonhoeffer's prediction of a "strong" secular population, Shoemaker saw that an increasing number of lives are out of control. No one in his generation developed a satisfactory general theory of addiction, but Shoemaker observed that many people experience inner forces they cannot control and "problems" they cannot manage, that destroy them over time, and from which they are powerless to free themselves.

In this sense of problems that are bigger than the people who have them, Shoemaker observed that "almost everyone has a problem, is a problem, or lives with a problem." The phenomenon he observed is even more widespread today. Many millions of people are addicted to some "substance"—from alcohol to nicotine to food to many drugs; additional millions have addictions to work, making money, sex, gambling, dependent relationships, or some other "process." So, many people's lives are out of control.

10. Secular people cannot find "the door"

Shoemaker also saw that people who are not disciples of Christ are "lost" and need to be found. They search for God, ultimate reality, and faith, but they cannot by themselves find "the most important door in the world," which is "the door through which people walk when they find God." The philosopher Unamuno contended that "those who deny God deny Him because of their despair at not finding Him."[25] In his celebrated poem, Shoemaker observed that people

> . . . crave to know where the door is.
> And all that so many ever find
> Is only a wall where a door ought to be.
> They creep along the wall like blind men,
> With outstretched, groping hands.
> Feeling for a door, knowing there must be a door,
> Yet they never find it. . . .

Men die outside that door, as starving beggars die
On cold nights in cruel cities in the dead of winter—
Die for want of what is within their grasp.
They live on the other side of it—
live because they have not found it.[26]

These ten characteristics of secular people are broad generalizations about many, if not most, secular people. They do not exhaust the generalizations we could venture about secular people, but they provide enough of a map of the territory to enable any church in the West to make sense of its mission field. Undoubtedly, some characteristics feed others; for instance, people with low self-esteem are more addiction prone. It is not unusual to find secular people who represent every feature of this profile.

Themes and Strategies for Reaching Secular People

*H*ow can we reach secular people and communicate the faith in the post-Christendom mission fields of the western world? The preceding profile implies a number of strategic ways forward. The themes and strategies in this chapter do not exhaust the possibilities for reaching people who fit the profile, but they demonstrate the usefulness of developing, and reflecting upon, a target population profile. Furthermore, these themes and strategies are not speculative; they are being used by communicators and congregations reaching secular people. Moreover, to these known strategies for reaching secular people, we can confidently add the principles established in church-growth research for reaching any population in the world.

1. Provide ministries of instruction

If secular people are largely ignorant of basic Christianity, then the ministry of instruction becomes necessary in reaching them. Donald Soper discovered, in years of fielding questions in the open air, that the christian communicator must repeatedly answer one question: " 'What is Christianity?' That is precisely what the outsider doesn't know, so the advocate must be prepared to explain, over and over, what Christianity is, stands for, and offers—rather than what people take it to be." Soper faults most christian teachers for "beginning in the middle" and presupposing the basics which most secular people do *not* understand. Soper explains that "it may sound trite, but, if only impassioned evangelists would tell the story of Jesus Christ, what he said, how he lived and died and what happened to those who were his disciples, if they would concentrate upon those primary elements in the christian religion and proclaim them as if they were unfolding a new and unheard Gospel, they would over and over again be breaking virgin ground.''[1]

Two rules of thumb inform basic christian instruction today. First, it is okay to make it interesting—and thereby retain people's attention! Second, people learn more effectively through participation than by passively receiving information. There are pioneers in the ministry of instruction to secular people, notably in Australia. David Robinson, of the United Church of Australia's Board of Mission, reports the instructional effectiveness of involving people who do not yet believe in christian music and drama.

Another approach in Australia organizes people into studies of Mark's Gospel, using the instructor's manual *Christianity Explained* by Michael Bennett.[2] The manual is based upon three bold principles. First, assume they know nothing; not even the identity of King David or Simon Peter. Second, do not ask them to read aloud in the group or to pray aloud or to answer questions about the Bible or Christianity; those very fears almost kept them from joining the study group. Third, proceed slowly. Inviting a response after a single presentation is now impossible. They are usually ready to respond in the fifth or sixth week of a six-week course; one in two or three persons responds in commitment.

2. *Invite people to dedicate their lives*

Sam Shoemaker agrees that too many christian spokesmen falsely presuppose, and omit, basic Christianity, adding that christian interpreters also characteristically omit inviting people to decisively and radically commit their lives to basic Christianity. He observed that the average minister is trying to help people to continue something they have not yet begun, which is as illogical as telling people how to get a second wind or round the far turn in a race they have not yet decided to run! ''The average person in the pews has never been told how to make Christian experience a fact instead of an aspiration. Many so-called Christian people have never definitely, in any clearcut and decisive way, begun their Christian life.''

The state of the Church at the present time, its place of low esteem in the mind of the outsider, its impotence in the affairs of the world, its level of complacent contentment with a little round of pious duties, is witness enough that we are in . . . an age of spiritual powerless and decline. . . . It is my contention that the trouble goes back to the very start, or rather to the want of any conclusive start at all.[3]

3. Help secular people find meaning

If secular people today are less obsessed with life after death and more obsessed with life this side of death, then the church that helps people make sense of their life and find meaning for their life will be scratching where many people itch. Indeed, Dean M. Kelley's *Why Conservative Churches Are Growing* basically contends that the communication of life's meaning is the central and indispensable function of the christian religion.[4] Churches that do not help people make sense of their lives and find meaning and purpose are neglecting their essential mission.

4. Engage secular people in dialogue

If conscious doubt, not conscious guilt, is now the number one factor in a secular population, what strategy is appropriate? Traditionally, the Church has relied on authoritative preaching to reach the unchurched masses, but most secular people experience such preaching as *authoritarian* preaching. It turns them off, or they are merely amused by the "great pulpit oratory" that many church people still love. Rick Warren, in a private interview, suggests that there are no more "great orators." The speakers who get a hearing today "engage in animated conversation," like Johnny Carson or Ronald Reagan. Warren offers this advice to would-be communicators to the secular mind: "Decide that you are going to be a communicator, not a commentator. . . . TV has permanently altered the attention span of Americans, so get right to the point. . . . If you are going to quote someone, don't quote some dead Englishman. Quote Rosanne Barr or Bill Cosby."

The most proven approach for engaging secular people at the point of their doubts is dialogue. Donald Soper's open-air forums represent one viable form of dialogue. (The rough equivalent, in the United States, of the British open-air meeting is the "radio call-in show.") Samuel Shoemaker's "interviews" with doubting people represent another.[5] Reasonable caring conversations with secular seekers are already achieving more than the Church knows, and the approach could be multiplied in every community in the West.

My own fairly extensive dialogical ministry with doubting people has generated four important discoveries. First, if you engage in honest open dialogue with people at the point of their honest doubts, you will give some satisfying answers! God has not left you intellectually abandoned; your years of study and reflection actually yield some answers that can help people, and remove some barriers between them and the leap of faith!

Second, you will discover, in such dialogue, that you do *not* have adequate answers to some of the questions people ask. This discovery will drive you to your Bible and your knees, and to many more relevant theological discoveries than one finds in mere "desk theology."

Third, in such dialogue, the evangelist should be honest about his or her doubts, as well as his or her faith. Doubt is part of the human condition, and all of us have been tarred with secularity's brush. The evangelist is *primarily* listening, probing, sharing available answers, and confessing faith, but one is also identifying with the struggler and sharing that one knows how doubt feels. Many times, people need to be informed that it is okay to become a Christian before all of one's doubts are resolved!

Fourth, often the very process of unthreatening dialogue with a caring nonjudgmental Christian is a liberating experience. Often, after people have named and shared their doubts, the doubts are "defanged," no longer tyrannizing their souls; and they are able to risk the experiment of faith—bringing their doubts with them. But helping people with doubts find faith is a longer process than helping people seeking forgiveness. Soper observed that "guilt is like tinder that blazes when the spark of emotion is applied to it, whereas doubt is like a rust which can only be removed by careful polishing."[6]

5. *Address secular people's doubts and questions*

If secular people doubt the Church's capacity to know and teach ultimate Truth, the Church is called to clarify its truth claims and develop an apologetic that responds to people's questions and makes sense to inquiring minds. Donald Morgan's book, *How to Get It Together When Your World Is Coming Apart,* addresses some of the very questions about God that secular searching people most often pose—such as "Does God exist?" "What is God like?" "Can we know God?" "Does God know us?" "Is God involved with us?" and "Can we believe in miracles in a scientific age?"[7]

6. *Provide opportunities to meet credible Christians*

Since the credibility of Christians and the Church is a question for secular people, they need to meet credible Christians. I have observed, as a church consultant, that God is not without witness in any church; there are some people in every church who experience grace, who love God and other people, and are transparently credible. The wise church will know that Christianity is "more caught than taught," and will arrange the kinds of social occasions in which seekers can meet credible Christians, study their faces, ask questions, and be in their company.

Sam Shoemaker organized Thursday Evening Groups for this explicit purpose. Such a Group features laypeople who are presently conducting "the experiment of faith," who honestly share their struggles and discoveries:

The outsider . . . understands it when a bad man turns good, or when a good man shakes off his self-satisfaction and becomes Christian. He understands it when a man on the road to nowhere finds a direction toward a destiny, or when a life adrift comes into harbour—he understands and he likes it, and he says in the soul of him: "Now, that's what I call Christianity."[8]

One of Shoemaker's "cases" in *Children of the Second Birth* reports "a man in whom inferiority had become . . . ingrained." He heard Shoemaker speak at Princeton, and migrated to New York to attach to Trinity Church and explore the christian possibility. At first, he came because the people believed and were undergoing transforming experiences. Then "he decided to try Christianity—*real* Christianity, experimentally. One day he began getting 'guidance'. . . . When he went home for vacation, things were different."[9]

Likewise, a restless, half-converted woman of privilege, following a serious illness, came to a Thursday Evening Group. She saw "a light and a joy" in the faces of some of the people; she sensed reality in the atmosphere. After several days of fighting, she "surrendered" to Christ, and "miracles began to happen in and through her" as she straightened some things from her past, experienced release from hatred, and peace amidst pain.[10]

7. Provide opportunities for people to overcome alienation

Urban church leaders, who know that many secular people are alienated from nature, know to plan retreats in natural settings that enable people to get in touch with God's natural revelation.

Church leaders who know that secular people are often alienated from their neighbors promote small groups, including support groups for seekers. Donald Soper observed, early in his open-air ministry, that "only in a vital Christian fellowship will God become real to most people. . . . The key to the problem of modern day agnosticism is fellowship. Out of the failure of Christian fellowship it has emerged, and in the recovery of a Christian fellowship it will give place once again to faith and assurance."[11]

Church leaders who know that many secular people are alienated from the political and economic powers upon which their lives depend will join evangelism with christian social causes, and will invite alienated people to join Christians in working for justice. Indeed, evangelism has a greater stake in justice causes than evangelicals usually perceive. William Temple saw that "social witness is both a preparation for evangelism and a consequence of it." Social witness and social reform are a preparation for evangelism because the life experience of persons living in a supportive, just, and humane environment condition them to trust the message that the universe is friendly.

The fact that a people's social experience and perceptions influence their capacity to believe the Word of God is documented as early as Exodus 6. Moses proclaims to the people that the Lord their God has heard their groaning and will redeem them and give them a land, but the people "did not listen to Moses, because of their broken spirit and their cruel bondage" (Exodus 6:9). Likewise, an environment of poverty, hunger, violence, war, sensualism, and materialism make it difficult for people to hear the Word of God. Nevertheless, the practical work of evangelism must be done in each season in the milieu in which people live, because we cannot afford the luxury of waiting for a more favorable set of conditions; so we work in the present social conditions to convert sufficient persons to work for the more just and humane society that will make it more possible for more people to believe.

Church leaders who know that many secular people are alienated from their jobs will rediscover the Protestant doctrine of vocation and interpret it to a new generation.

Christians who are especially aware of the loneliness of alienated people will engage in empathetic identification and relational honesty. Bruce Larson observes that "we are all lonely people. Everybody goes through life single. . . . We are all lonely people, married or single. Really, all you have when you get done is Jesus. 'I will never leave you nor forsake you.' Everybody else can leave or forsake you." Furthermore, Larson warns that a garbled response to the gospel will leave us lonely. The Bible invites us to "trust God and love people." The devil twists this truth and influences us to "love God and trust people." Larson warns that "if you do that, you will wind up bitter," because "we are going to fail each other. We try not to, but we will." So, "trust God and love people. We still give ourselves away for people. Don't stop loving, but only trust God."

8. Engage in ministries of affirmation

Church leaders who know that many secular people are untrusting will engage in ministries of affirmation. Robert Schuller observes that part of this point is negative. In relating to secular seekers, we must be careful to not insult them, demean them, or come across as better than them. Positively, the ministry of affirmation requires the

61

socioemotional maturity to not take personally their expressions of distrust, and it requires spending time with them, affirming them, and managing affirming experiences for them. Given time and affirming experiences, insecure people will learn to trust more. Schuller reports that many secular people need to know in advance that they will not be rejected, or insulted, or humiliated, or walk into a setup. " 'Unsaved souls'—insecure, nontrusting persons—will need a great deal of positive affirmation before they will be able to 'listen' and 'hear' and begin to comprehend the truth of saving grace.'' [12]

9. Help people discover their dignity and self-worth

If many secular people have low self-esteem, this means that the doctrine of creation—that people are created in God's image, with dignity and for significant responsibility—is part of the good news that the Christian movement must now communicate. The New Testament gospel presupposes this truth about humanity which, in western culture, has been forgotten and must now be an explicit part of the message. Unfortunately, the sequence of most evangelistic messages today is "Bad News, Good News." We are called to recover the full biblical sequence of "Good News, Bad News, Good News." Scripture begins with the good creation (not with the fall), and so must we.

Robert Schuller believes that people must first discover their dignity and self-worth before they can become the kind of converts that the christian movement needs. To convert people who still feel bad about themselves "is like baptizing people in a swamp"; it qualifies them for heaven, but they become emotionally handicapped Christians, and some become ministers and perpetuate the syndrome. It is hard to graduate from negative Christianity. Schuller believes that it is possible to appeal to the positive worth and value that remains in secular people, though they are lost sinners, and help them to believe in their dignity and worth as the threshold experience to positive christian conversion.

If Bruce Larson is right that most people are from dysfunctional families and are deceived about their own identity and worth, then the Church is the new Family of God given for people searching for their true identity. One especially discovers within a small group, through voluntary disclosure and walking in the light, that "My gosh, I'm not what my parents said. The sun and stars do not revolve around me; nor am I junk.'' In such a group, the seeker can find ''people with some detachment and commitment, who will love me, call forth my gifts, and give me a new name, and I will see myself in their eyes and discover who I am.'' Larson believes that people also discover who they are from ''involvement in hands-on mission and ministry to high school kids, to homeless people, to drug addicts—to some-body. . . . So mission is not just to help the world; it's also that you might find who you are, and do some good along the way!''

10. Offer people hope in the Kingdom of God

If many secular people see history as out of control and fear the future, the christian doctrine of the Kingdom of God—with its promised consummation and Second Coming of Christ, and the related doctrine of Providence, is a dimension of the biblical revelation that needs to be interpreted meaningfully to this insecure generation. Ken Chafin observes that, unfortunately, much of the Church has

taken the doctrine of the Second Coming—which is a very valid New Testament doctrine, and turned it into an esoteric doctrine, and turned it over to the crazies and the confused Zionists. We have failed to realize that the doctrine, originally perceived, was the doctrine of Hope. The doctrine rightly communicates the confidence that the Creator God who came in Christ is still in charge of the universe; it's not out of control, and He will bring it to conclusion and fulfill His purposes and promises. I think that if you can undress the doctrine of the Second Coming from all the gaudy clothes it has picked up, it has a far more significant appeal to secular people than anyone realizes.

11. Provide support groups for people with addictions

If many secular people are addicted and not in control of their lives, then the ''12-Step Movement'' is here to stay and has a growing future. Indeed, there is evidence that the 12-Step Movement is the ''underground revival of the 1990s,'' that more people are now experiencing the empowering grace of God in 12-Step groups than in all of the more visible evangelism programs combined!

Alcoholics Anonymous, and its many spinoff 12-Step programs for other addictions, was launched under Samuel Shoemaker in New York City, when Calvary Episcopal Church started Calvary Mission as "A place where a Carpenter still mends broken men." The 12-Step movement must be welcomed more fully into the ministries of more churches than ever before. No other organization has the opportunity to facilitate the number of 12-Step Groups that are needed in western society. Art Glasser contends that "addiction" is the dominant form that possessive and destructive Evil has taken today in our culture. The Church is called to represent the compassionate power of *Christus Victor* to the millions of addiction-possessed people of this generation. As one example, Schuller's Crystal Cathedral is now pioneering in ministries to addicted people. That church offers ministries and support groups for alcoholics, adult children of alcoholics, Al-Anon, "women who love too much," men prone to violence, Addictions Anonymous, Gamblers Anonymous, Narcotics Anonymous, and Overeaters Anonymous.

Viable strategies for reaching secular people are also present in much of what we know in church-growth lore about how the Church grows and how the faith spreads in any population.[13] Although Kenneth Chafin does not represent the church-growth school of thought, I will show that his extensive experience and observations have corroborated its chief insights, thereby demonstrating that the following church-growth principles are useful whether or not one "buys" the whole church-growth package.

12. *Identify and reach receptive people*

Secular people experience receptive seasons in their lives, when they are dissatisfied with their lives, when the prevenient grace of God is moving in their souls, when they are open to "something else" and when communication to them is more possible. Churches who pray to be led to people whom God is preparing and who employ church-growth guidelines for identifying likely receptive people will experience harvest among populations even in North America or Europe. Kenneth Chafin counsels "the reluctant witness" to learn that "we are not being sent out to a hostile world into which God has not gone. We are invited to *follow* him into his world and bear witness."[14]

13. *Reach across social networks*

Secular people can be reached better by credible Christians in their kinship and friendship networks than by christian strangers. The social networks between believers and nonchristians, especially between new believers and nonchristians, provide the christian movement with what Donald McGavran called "the bridges of God." Churches who coach their people to reach the unchurched secular people in their social networks of relatives, friends, neighbors, and colleagues will find more of them receptive than the Church would guess. However, outreach across each of these types of networks does not take place the same way or involve the same kind of experience. Communicating the faith to a close relative is often difficult, and the experience can be clumsy because, as Ken Chafin observes, "We often get so emotionally involved in our witness to people we love that the intensity comes through, but the love does not." Chafin reports that

the most difficult witness I ever bore in my life was to my father. I was twenty-five years old and he was forty-five. I had been a Baptist preacher for several years. My father was living in Kansas and came to spend a week with me when I was preaching in a little church in northeastern Oklahoma. . . .

Now if you had asked me to talk to *your* father I could have done it easily. But every time I would open my mouth to try to talk to my father about Jesus all I could think of was the things I had done that had hurt my father. And so finally I just said, "Dad, I want you to know that I'm terribly sorry for anything that I've ever done to hurt you." That was as far as I got. I started crying. I never did get to talk to him about becoming a Christian. But that night my father committed his life to Jesus Christ.[15]

Reaching a close family member is often difficult, and this case illustrates some of the usual dynamics. First, the Holy Spirit prepared Chafin's father to respond. Second, his dad observed the Christ-induced changes in Ken's life. Third, the Holy Spirit enabled Chafin to communicate more than he was able to verbalize. Fourth, Chafin's church in northeastern Oklahoma provided a warm climate for a seeker and welcomed him into its fellowship even before he believed. Often, the christian family member will plant the seed, and perhaps water it over time, but some other person or group from the church will have to invite the seeker and gather the harvest.

By contrast, sharing the gospel across friendship networks is more manageable, and outreach across friendship networks can produce more new Christians than any other outreach mode. The faith, of course, does not spread automatically along a believer's kinship and friendship networks; it requires our intentional efforts in other people's behalf. Spreading the faith demands that we maintain our friendships with nonchristians. Ken Chafin reminds us that sometimes we are embarrassed around people "who knew us when," and that it is all too easy "to unconsciously build a world made up entirely of fellow Christians."[16]

In many communities, even greater intentionality is required. Willow Creek Community Church has discovered that, in the Chicago area, there are many unchurched people who are not already in a relationship with any credible faith-sharing Christian. They are insulated from the influence of Christianity, and the usual approaches to evangelism such as bumper stickers, TV evangelists, radio spots, and tracts will miss or alienate them. Reaching such people begins when Christians "build credible, integrity-filled relationships" with unchurched people—at work, in the neighborhood, in schools and clubs.

14. Offer culturally appropriate forms of ministry

Secular people, like any tribe in Africa, are reached more effectively through the people, language, liturgy, music, architecture, needs, struggles, issues, leaders, and leadership style that are indigenous to their culture. We know that this cardinal principle of christian mission applies to other mission fields, of course, but have not yet discovered its necessary application to our western fields, because we haven't thought of what we do as "foreign" to unchurched people in the West. But Kenneth Chafin was suggesting, a quarter century ago, that unchurched seekers experience our buildings, liturgies, stained-glass windows, organ music, ushers, offering plates, and ''our people with their Sunday faces on'' as culturally alien, bizarre, and even intimidating.[17]

My own interviews with secular seekers who visited a church, but didn't join or return, have surfaced a widespread fear that the church wants to make them like ''church people.'' The barrier, as they explain it, is not theological but cultural; but they can only deal with the gospel when they have somehow worked through the cultural barrier—or when a ''seeker sensitive church'' has cared enough to remove it. Typically, when secular people experience ''church'' as culturally alien to them, they assume that the christian God is not for people like them; they believe they have to learn to dress, talk, tote Bibles, and genuflect like the Christians do, before God will accept them.

This barrier is tragic, because through the Jerusalem Council that is reported in Acts 15, the early Church supposedly settled this matter once and for all. The first church council decided that Gentiles did *not* have to become culturally Jewish (be circumcised, give up pork, etc.) before they could become disciples of Christ. Over time, we have forgotten this important lesson—to the detriment of our mission. Many unchurched people today assume, say, that learning to pray in Elizabethan English and to enjoy eighteenth-century German pipe organ music is a prerequisite to relating to Christ. But Jesus said he did not come to destroy the cultures of the peoples of the earth, but to fulfill them! And we now know that the christian revelation can be mediated through any culture on earth, which demonstrates Christianity to be a universal faith. For Christianity, each people's culture is the most appropriate, and potent, medium for God's revelation to them, so the caring christian movement develops an indigenous (or contextualized) church for each culture.

Alan Walker advocates ''the contextualization of the gospel *everywhere*, as Paul did for the Hellenistic world,'' because he has observed that where Christianity's forms are contextualized, ''it is indigenized and growing much more.'' But where the forms are foreign to the host culture, ''it is dead and largely failing.'' He believes that there has never been a great christian awakening or movement in Australia because ''we've yet to develop forms that are indigenous to Australian culture''; Australian Christianity is felt, at least, to be totally borrowed from Great Britain and North America, and therefore ''foreign.'' He stresses that Christianity everywhere is rooted in "the same gospel" and is, in fact, the one demonstrated "universal faith," but it must be contextualized for every people and culture.

The extent to which the faith is likely indigenized for a given culture is most obviously observed in the Church's music and the people's spontaneous, contagious, celebrative involvement in the music. Indeed, Eugene Nida observes that "all creative and extensive periods of church growth have been characterized by an appropriate indigenous hymnody."[18]

Curiously, the Church's language represents an overlooked area for indigenization in the West. C. S. Lewis argued that a clergy candidate's capacity to translate theology into common English ought to be a test for ordination. He remarked that "it is absolutely disgraceful that we expect our missionaries to the Bantus to learn Bantu, but never ask whether our missionaries to the Americans or the English can speak American or English. Any fool can write *learned* language. The vernacular is the real test. If you can't turn your faith into the vernacular, then either you don't understand it or you don't believe it."[19]

15. Multiply "units" of the Church

New units—that is, new classes, new groups, new choirs, and new congregations—will disciple more secular people than will old units, because secular people are more interested in getting in on the start of something, where everybody is "even," than in joining an established group with cliques and a fixed agenda. Ken Chafin has long championed the planting of new churches in a denomination's strategy for reaching people, because at least 70 percent of the people who join a new church join as new believers, and at least 70 percent of those converts could not have been won by established churches. So, Chafin says, "Show me a denomination that has stopped planting new churches, and I will show you a denomination that is already in a terminal condition." He has also championed the Sunday school as evangelism's "secret weapon," and has shown how Sunday schools grow largely through the proliferation of new Sunday school classes—created as recruiting groups and ports of entry for new people. Some churches stress the "multiplication of units" principle even more extravagantly, as they reach new people through multiplying new worshiping congregations, choirs, Bible study groups, support groups, ministries, human services, and activities.

Rick Warren thus refers to Saddleback Valley's ''Trotline'' evangelism philosophy: ''The more hooks you use, the more fish you are going to catch!'' And new hooks can catch and hold more fish than old hooks. According to Warren, ''All new growth grows faster than old growth; so you have to create new units within old churches for those to grow.'' Part of Warren's rationale for multiplying units is to give people options. He has observed, with Ray Bakke, that the supermarket which stocked 8,000 items and closed at 10:00 P.M. ten years ago will offer twice as many products today—including Spanish, Asian, and dietetic aisles, 24 hours a day. Yet the church down the street still offers its one 11:00 worship service, offers no more options than twenty years ago, and wonders why a generation expecting options is passing them by! So Saddleback Valley Community Church offers multiple services, multiple types of small groups, multiple ministries, and multiple ways of coming to Christ, because ''very few people will be put on a conveyor belt today, and say we are all going to do the same thing, at the same time, every day of the week.''

16. Offer ministries that meet needs

Secular people are more reachable through ministries that engage their struggles, felt needs, and driving motives. The strategy of ministering to a range of human needs is the main way that churches demonstrate Christianity's ''relevance,'' which is necessary precisely because so many secular people assume the faith to be irrelevant to the real struggles that people and communities experience. So churches who develop ministries that ''scratch where people itch'' will engage and disciple more of them.

Kenneth Chafin observes that secular people express very religious needs (though in nonreligious language) such as the need for meaning and purpose in life, the need for significance, the need to make a contribution, the need to be needed, the need to make sense of my life, and the need to come to terms with mortality. Because people do ask these questions, these questions and needs provide a ''point of contact'' for the gospel. Chafin perceives that "there is an easier point of contact out there than I thought at an earlier time in my life." He has learned that often we can engage those points of contact more effectively through ministry than through evangelism that is apart from ministry. The available point of contact is a point of felt need, which may be engaged by, say, a seminar for people with failed marriages, or a clinic for immigrants who are outside the health delivery system, or a grief recovery group. Chafin believes that "the church that is unwilling to minister to persons probably will not stay in business. The authentic church needs to minister as well as articulate a gospel."

Part of reaching secular people involves developing a relevant credible local church which transparently cares and is involved in the lives of people and the life of the community. But our outreach should not involve an apologetic for the whole Church because, as Ken Chafin confesses, "the Church has been so slow and so wrong on so many issues, that you could spend all your time apologizing for it." A local church can nevertheless become a faithful relevant church, and sell that church, its mission and openness, to seeking people. Once secular people become disciples inside that church, they will in time discover and experience much good about the whole Church, and will come to love it, warts and all. But you do not begin effectively by trying to sell the whole Church to secular people.

The principle of meeting needs should inform teachers and preachers of the faith. My interviews revealed that every effective communicator with secular people knows this and works at this. Soper, for example, reports that "whatever else happens at Speakers' Corner or on Tower Hill, one thing is certain: you are heard only if you are relevant."[20] So Soper typically begins an open-air meeting addressing a need or problem reflected in the news that day, or at the point of people's quest for meaning, peace, or economic justice.

Donald Morgan observes that the secular people of New England live in "the two worlds of psychology and technology." The christian comunicator will either "talk to the world as they know it" or reinforce their assumption that Christians live in an ivory tower. Busy people will not waste time on what seems to be irrelevant. Morgan joins Schuller, Leslie Weatherhead, and others in believing that the gospel can be communicated at least as adequately today in psychology's terms as it was in the Middle Ages in juridical terms. So

70

he typically positions the gospel to illuminate people's struggles—employing the familiar terms of "pop psychology." The title of his book, *How to Get It Together When Your World Is Coming Apart,* serves as an example. The book devotes chapters to common human experiences like pain, anger, worry, depression, fear, aging, "keeping your cool," and the temptation to quit.

Rick Warren also observes that secular people describe their condition with terms from pop psychology—such as "My life is out of control" or "I am falling apart." Furthermore, when a secular person suddenly shows up in church, she or he may bring expectations similar to those for a hospital's emergency ward; they are looking for help now. Warren speculates that "the person in the emergency ward isn't interested in the Latin word for 'tapioca.' " Warren has learned that the most effective approach to preaching and teaching from the Scriptures is not verse-by-verse exposition, but "topical exposition"—in which the speaker addresses a theme like stress, loneliness, marriage relationships, the search for meaning or purpose, or dealing with crises or things that are out of control.

Warren once preached a series on the Seven Deadly Sins—without ever using those traditional terms. He featured the series as "Breaking Free From the Habits and Hangups That Are Messing Up Your Life." The sermon on "Greed" raised the serious questions in ways familiar to secular people, such as "Why do I always feel like I have to have more? No matter how much I get, I have to have more! Why do I have that feeling?" Then Warren shared the biblical understanding behind this nearly universal experience: "That I think that getting more is going to bring me security or satisfaction."

Some communicators, like Kenneth Chafin, enable people to identify with a person or situation described in a biblical passage, and thereby see the message's relevance for them. Chafin's sermon series out of the life of David, a transparently human Old Testament character, serves as a model.[21] For instance, in the story of the death of David's son Absalom, Chafin saw that, due to guilt and grief, David could not get over this loss. Like David, most of us have something in our past that immobilizes us, that we can't get over. Again, in the episode where David is ready to build the temple in Jerusalem—but God prohibits its construction for now—David experienced the death of his life's dream. Most people have this same experience, when they realize they will not accomplish what they had planned. Again, Chafin saw that the greatest development experiences in David's life were not experienced during his time in the palace, but rather during his years as a fugitive in exile. We therefore see "What to Do with the Down Periods of Your Life," as David models the principle of salvaging a future out of the bad things that happen to us.

17. Engage secular people on "their turf"

Finally, if secular people are lost and cannot find the door to faith, then the secular West needs a generation of many Christians willing to "stand by the door" with Samuel Shoemaker. He declared, "I stand by the door [to faith in God]. I neither go too far in, nor stay too far out." Shoemaker admired the many Christians who go deeply into the riches and depth of the Christian community, experience, and fellowship, who become saints and enjoy the other saints of God. But he preferred his "old accustomed place" by the door—

Near enough to God to hear Him, and know He is there,
But not so far from people as to not hear them—Outside the door.[22]

In the mission fields of North America and Europe, we must challenge great numbers of churches to turn from good church work to do the Work of the Church. Shoemaker needs more company in the apostolic ministry of "standing by the door."

Communicating with Secular People

*W*e have inherited the ancient expectation in Isaiah 55—that God sent forth the Word for a purpose, desiring not that it should return to God void but accomplish this purpose—that people will seek the Lord while God may be found, and receive God's covenant that their souls may live; and when people do turn to God "all the trees of the field will clap their hands" (vs. 12). For this purpose God sent the Word. But we know, through 2 Corinthians 5, that God does not rescue people unilaterally, but with the involvement of the People of God who are already reconciled. God makes us Christ's ambassadors, entrusts us with the message of reconciliation, and makes "his appeal through us" (vs. 20).

The question that increasingly haunts God's ambassadors in North America and Europe is "How do we effectively communicate the message of reconciliation and life to the secular unchurched people who have no christian background, memory, or vocabulary, the millions of 'ignostics' who do not know what we are talking about?" We are learning that this is a complex communication challenge, and there is no available magic, or panacea, or quick fix, or any evangelistic formula that cuts through all of the complexity. We recall that, indeed, "no one can say 'Jesus is Lord' except by the Holy Spirit" (1 Cor. 12:3). We are rediscovering that if we will love "the Lord of the harvest" with our minds, as well as with our hearts, the Holy Spirit will often communicate through our best efforts.

What insights and models are available to help inform our ministry to secular unchurched people?

COMMUNICATION DYNAMICS

As the grace of God is mediated in the sacraments through the water, bread, and wine, so God's Word is communicated through the regular dynamics of human communication. As Charles G. Finney observed, God's revelation to people does not usually suspend the "laws" of the human mind and human audience, but occurs through those laws.[1] Actually, Augustine was the first to perceive that the christian communicator needs to learn secular communication theory to better communicate christian truth. Augustine believed that all knowledge could serve the christian cause, including communication theory. Using a metaphor from Exodus, he recommended that the christian preacher and teacher "plunder the Egyptians . . . for their gold."[2] Augustine taught us to not regard the gospel's communication as a more unique challenge than it is, or ourselves as less prepared than we are. The most proven models of communication and persuasion can help inform our communication with the Church and with secular people. Furthermore, since western society is now a competitive arena for many religions, movements, and ideologies, and since the public's expectations of all communicators have been raised in the media age, the only Christians who will be taken seriously will be informed communicators. While we cannot do full justice to communication theory within this project, I feature one communication model.

Aristotle's rhetorical model of communication has proven useful for twenty-three centuries.[3] Aristotle studied effective communicators and unpacked the three common components involved in effective communication. He observed three variables involved in all persuasion—the communicator, the message, and the audience, with appropriate adaptation to the setting or context. More specifically, his model shows that persuasion takes place in an interplay between the *ethos* of the communicator, the *logos* of the message, and the *pathos* of the audience.

By the *ethos* of the communicator, Aristotle referred to three characteristics of the communicator—intelligence, character, and good will, as perceived by the audience. He observed that people tend to be persuaded of the truth of the communicator's message when they perceive the communicator to be informed, moral, and interested in the audience's welfare. Later research in the *ethos* of the communicator has uncovered additional operating factors—like the audience's experience of the communicator's energy or dynamism, and the audience's perception of the communicator's credibility, and the degree to which the audience likes the communicator.

In discussing the *logos* of the message, Aristotle observed that the message must make sense to the audience. Primarily he was making a case for good reasons and sound arguments. Aristotle also stressed the importance of organizing a message to enable people to follow it, and he taught the features of a communicator's language style that could make the message clear, interesting, or even moving in the audience's experience.

By the *pathos* of the audience, Aristotle referred to the emotional state of the audience. In knowing, say, that people respond differently when they are angry than they do when they are amused, Aristotle taught the communicator how to identify, or influence, the emotional state of the audience, and thereby give the message a fair chance of acceptance. He also saw something of the role of the audience's felt needs and driving motives in persuasion, features more fully developed in persuasion studies today.[4]

The fields informing communication have advanced since Aristotle, but we still stand on Aristotle's shoulders, and his model is invaluable to christian advocates to secular populations. Specifically, Aristotle's identification of the three crucial components in the communication process—communicator, message, and audience, will prove perennially useful for planning effective communication and for diagnosing failures in communication. For instance, we have already suggested that Christianity's message may be rejected because of the auditor's low perception of the Church's ethos, or because the Church's message is not clear, or because its language is not indigenous to the target population. One must especially be aware that an effective communication event occurs through the synergism of a number of communication principles, seldom through one principle alone. Notice, for instance, how the following brief case from Kenneth Chafin's *The Reluctant Witness* illustrates the factors of ethos, pathos, and logos in reaching a cultured and widely traveled Mexican woman:

When I asked through the interpreter what caused her to believe, this is the story she told. "I came to this city as a stranger and I was very lonely. One of the ladies in your church came to visit me. At Christmas she brought me a book as a gift, and she even wrapped it in pretty paper. But the best thing was that she had me in her home for a meal. When I saw the very genuine love she had for me, I knew that the story in the book about God's love was true."[5]

THE "ADOPTION PROCESS"

When people adopt the christian message, the process by which they will reach that point will resemble the process, and stages, by which people adopt any new truth, practice, or life-style. A rich behavioral science research tradition has focused on the "diffusion of innovations," that is, the study of how new ideas, technologies, practices, and causes spread from person to person in a given society.[6] One promising set of insights from this research involves the "adoption process," the process in stages by which people typically adopt a new possibility. The data from christian conversions, I believe, would modify the diffusion research conclusions to permit us to delineate six stages people experience in adopting Christianity:

1. awareness
2. relevance
3. interest
4. trial
5. adoption
6. reinforcement

The meaning of each stage is almost self-evident from the labels. First, people become aware, or newly aware, of Christianity—not as an abstraction but as a particular movement, group of people, church, or truth claim. Second, people perceive the relevance of that perceived form of Christianity for some unmet felt need or driving motive in their life, their group, or their society. They respond, third, with active interest, in which they (perhaps) ask questions, read a book, attend a seminar, or visit a church's worship service. Fourth, they enter upon a trial stage, in which they consider the possibility, imagine what life would be like if they adopted, and perhaps engage in coffee conversations as though they were already Christians; in various ways, they are trying it on for size. Fifth, they consciously adopt the faith, and are publicly baptized and/or received into church membership at a particular time and place. Sixth, people, after adopting, typically experience a period of uncertainty or ambiguity about what has happened to them, during which they seek experiences that reinforce their decision and confirm their experience. Typically, discipling ministries and the church's liturgy will provide reinforcement, and new friendships, meaningful group involvement, and discovery of their gifts and involvement in ministry will confirm their experience and decision.

Such an understanding of the adoption process, though briefly stated, provides some needed handles for more effective communication of Christianity to secular people. The model of adoption helps us identify the two stages, trial and adoption, in which we are likely to see some visible response. The model helps us see why some people who respond at the trial stage may not be around later. The model helps us see the need for reinforcing our new converts and confirming them over some months into the christian community, scriptures, and ministries. The model will sensitize us to find out, through interviews, where people are in this process so our communication can begin where they are. Furthermore, when we know that people seldom work through that whole process in minutes or hours, but usually weeks or months, we are sensitized to work with people at a natural pace, to help people (for now) to the next stage, and not run ahead—and abort—the process leading to new life in God's good time.

The insights represented in adoption theory are not brand new to the christian movement. Some reflective evangelicals reach out with an understanding consistent with adoption theory. For instance, Canon Bryan Green maintains that there are at least four prerequisites for conversion:

First, paralleling the stage of awareness in adoption theory, Green observes that many secular people lack a sense of God or the transcendent, so "a pre-requisite of conversion is often a sense of the supernatural."[7] In Birmingham, England's St. Martin's in the Bull Ring, Green developed a three fold strategy for helping secular visitors to discover a God-consciousness: First, church architecture can rouse a sense of mystery, wonder, or the numinous. Second, a seeker's participation in a congregation of worshiping, praising, praying believers may suggest God's presence. Third, Canon Green typically ended his sermons with a period of "sacramental silence" when "God does His business with us." Green reasons that

> we cannot argue people into God, nor bludgeon them, nor even persuade them; they must encounter God for themselves—and why not in silence? In my missions as well as in my ordinary church preaching, my usual custom is, after the preaching of the Gospel, to have a period of silence. By this I mean real silence, not interrupted by the preacher, but a silence where there can be an encounter between the Divine and the human.[8]

But how do Christians stimulate this awareness in secular people who never darken the door of a church? My interviews with twenty of Green's first-generation converts reflected the following typical dynamics, with two or more usually operating in a person's life to help awaken him or her: Observing the serving work of the church in the community; observing the credibility of some Christians; friendship with Christians; open, nonthreatening, nonjudgmental conversations with one or more Christians; the witness or testimony of one or more Christians; the good sense reflected in Green's magazine columns or his speaking in the city; a personal invitation to visit the church—often multiple invitations, often to come with the inviter; and the friendliness of the people and the expectant atmosphere the visitor experienced in the church in the first few minutes. Green's strategy is consistent with this data from his converts. But Green observes that preaching cannot engage "the complete outsider," for whom "God is a meaningless symbol," who "feel no need of God. . . . The only strategy that offers us any hope of success with this man is for the Christian church to infiltrate the world."[9]

Green's second prerequisite for conversion corresponds to the stages of relevance and interest in adoption theory: the Church's communicators must demonstrate the christian message's relevance to the needs and motives that drive people's lives. Beyond what adoption theory requires, Green's communicator must also assist the Holy Spirit to convince the secular seeker that his or her need is, at least in part, a symptom of his or her alienation from God. One can sometimes demonstrate this deeper need for God by teaching the Law of God, or by comparing the seeker's character with the character of Christ, or by demonstrating the reality of corporate sin in the world, or by showing the crucifixion of Jesus as the consequence of people's sins.[10]

Attaining Green's third prerequisite for conversion, communication of some adequate "knowledge of Christ's life and work," becomes possible when the receiver is in the interest stage. Canon Green rejects William James' contention that a prior knowledge of Christ is not essential to conversion and also denies that "a complete dogmatic presentation of Christ" is necessary for conversion to occur. Green contends that a secular seeker must know enough about Christ "for something of what He reveals about God to make its appeal to the soul; some glimpse through Christ into the heart of God must capture the imagination before a person can be converted."[11]

Green's fourth prerequisite for conversion also parallels the interest stage in adoption theory. Even though conversion is the apostle's objective, "conversion does not happen when we talk about conversion."[12] If we preach conversion, the hearer experiences the message as a form of the Law, that is, something one must do to be justified. Rather, we facilitate conversion when we communicate the gospel of God's acceptance of us in Christ. "When Christ is lifted up," Christ's spirit attracts people to God and to the new life.

So, conversion is possible for a person when he or she senses the transcendent, feels a deep need for God, understands some gospel, and is focusing on Christ. The first three stages toward adoption—awareness, relevance, and interest—have been achieved. The evangelist then helps the seeker move to the trial stage by encouraging an "experiment of faith." Following a self-authenticating experiment, the evangelist can help the seeker move to the adoption stage by inviting the person to receive Christ's Spirit and become his disciple. This "challenge for a verdict" typically causes a "crisis" in the person, which is resolved by a decision, yea or nay. Green explains that "this 'crisis' is a crisis of choice and need not be an emotional experience or a dramatic conversion. But evangelism is not just offering the gospel in a 'take it or leave it' fashion"; it involves inviting a response.[13]

MISSIONARY PRINCIPLES

The effective communication of Christianity's good news in the post-Christendom era for the West will resemble all missionary communication challenges. Therefore, Lesslie Newbigin's threefold pattern for encountering any culture with the gospel is useful in encountering our own. Newbigin explains, in *Foolishness to the Greeks,* that missionary communication must take place: (1) In the language of the receptor culture—accepting "at least provisionally, the way of understanding things that is embodied in that language." (2) The missionary communication will call radically into question that culture's understanding of reality—with an appropriate call for repentance, in the sense of "a U-turn of the mind." (3) Missionary communicators know that when the receptor(s) discover faith and experience conversion, this is supremely to be attributed to a miracle, the work of God, and not primarily to the missionary's great theology or communication competency.[14] Newbigin adds that effective missionary communication always involves finding the path between two dangers:

On the one hand, he may simply fail to communicate: he uses the words of the language, but in such a way that he sounds like a foreigner; his message is heard as the babbling of a man who really has nothing to say. Or, on the other hand, he may so far succeed in talking the language of his hearers that he is accepted all too easily as a familiar character—a moralist calling for greater purity of conduct or a guru offering a path to the salvation that all human beings want. His message is simply absorbed into the existing world-view and heard as a call to be more pious or better behaved. In the attempt to be "relevant" one may fall into syncretism, and in the effort to avoid syncretism one may become irrelevant.[15]

There are, undoubtedly, other lessons to learn from the Church's extensive experience in missionary communication in many cultures. One lesson we once had to learn was not to impose American individualism upon other cultures. The view was that Americans and Europeans make decisions as individuals, so it is okay to invite people in the West to make individual decisions to be baptized and follow Christ. But in many cultures the individual is subordinated to the family, or clan, or tribe, or caste, or group (or to their company—as in Japan) to the point that their conscious identity is wrapped up with their group identity, and decisions get made by some group process. In such cultures, requiring individuals to decide for themselves is experienced as the requirement to leave their people and join another people—which, when they do it, can have tragic social consequences for them.[16]

We are now reviewing our assumptions about western individualism, and we are becoming more aware that many Westerners, too, have group loyalties and subculture identities, so that the differences between Westerners and Third World peoples is only in degree. Alan Walker, for one, reports to me that "in christian communication we have become crazy in our excessive individualism— trying to convert people out of their culture, social group, or friendship group, and put them into our group. That is a step many people are not prepared to make." He suggests that, in the western subcultures where it fits, we should do as we now know to do in India or Africa—and invite whole groups into faith and the Church! Some urban ministries to youth "gangs" and motorcycle gangs and seaport ministries to sailors are already demonstrating this possibility.

So, Christianity's communicators to secular people are already considerably fortified from the long tradition of communication theory, from the newer diffusion theory, and from mission theory, as well as the church-growth theory discussed earlier. No one has to start from scratch; we are not strategically naked in our vast, but complex, opportunity. Nevertheless, the data from converts, churches, apostolic pioneers and christian movements in our secular mission fields have blazed some promising new trails for the rest of us to follow. Let us look at four distinctively christian models for communicating with secular people; they are "breakout" models, departing from stereotypical evangelical methods in promising ways.

HOW SECULAR PEOPLE BECOME CHRISTIANS: FOUR MODELS

1. John Wesley's "Order of Salvation"

The first breakout model is John Wesley's "Order of Salvation." Wesley discovered in Great Britain's industrial revolution that the first generations of people moving to the cities had not maintained active connection with the Church, that the Church of England did not respond to urbanization by planting churches and deploying clergy to reach them, and so the next generations had not been reached and were as "secular" as any populations we face today. Wesley and the early Methodists faced populations with no christian memory and a negative attitude toward the Church. Wesley also apparently concluded that the two usual models for making Christians were both unproductive for these secular people—(1) the Anglican reliance upon rites of passage, and (2) the anabaptist model of communicating the message to people in the world and then, once converted, welcoming them into the Church. Both strategies, in Donald McGavran's words, "ought to work, but do not." In contrast to those models, Wesley reflected theologically, and upon his own experience, and he observed how some people were actually becoming Christians; he developed a distinctive four-step understanding of how to help secular urban people become Christians.[18]

The first step in Wesley's strategy is to "awaken" people to the knowledge of their lostness, to their need for God, to a desire to "flee the wrath to come" and experience a new life. The salient objective in Wesley's "field preaching" was to awaken people and get them started on the road to salvation. The objective of the Methodist people's ministry of witnessing was to awaken people.

Second, awakened people were always invited to enroll in a Methodist "class meeting," whether they yet believed anything or had yet experienced anything. The classes were lay led redemptive cells of 12 or fewer people.[19] If awakened persons desired to experience the grace of God and live a new life, they were invited to join a class. If they joined, and attended their weekly class meeting, and remained serious in their desire to live as a Christian and experience a new life, they were enrolled in the Methodist "society" three months later—whether or not they yet believed or experienced anything. Mr. Wesley seems to have perceived that Christianity is "more caught than taught," that seeking people are more likely to catch it from laity than from clergy, and cell life is even more indispensable than preaching in this contagion.

Third, each week they were coached to expect that they would in God's good time and way experience their justification. In most cases, where people remained earnestly seeking the new life, they experienced God's gracious acceptance. This experience usually occurred within several months to several years of their earlier awakening. It more usually happened in their solitude than in any other setting.

Fourth, once they had experienced their justification, they were coached to expect that, one day in this life, they would experience their sanctification—a second experience of God's grace in which they would completely surrender to God's will, be freed to live wholly by love, and become the people they were born to be. While most awakened people did experience their justification, most justified Methodist Christians, apparently, never experienced their sanctification—but they expected to, and this expectation energized the contagion and achievements of the Methodist movement.

Overall, Wesley's strategy seems to have been to replicate in other people the structure of his own experience, in which he tried for years to live as a Christian before becoming open to the grace of God that empowers people to live as Christians. The class meeting was, for a century, the characteristic institution that made possible Methodism's communication of christian reality to great numbers of people in both England and America, and Methodism still reaches many people through its multiplying class meetings in many Third World countries, particularly South Korea. So John Wesley's "Order of Salvation" is a widely proven model for reaching secular people in many lands and cultures.

2. Agnes Liu's "Triangle" scale

Another breakout model has been advanced in recent years by Agnes Liu of Hong Kong's China Graduate School of Theology, from the 16 years of a project studying and reaching out among working-class Chinese people who are secularized out of Chinese traditional religions. Dr. Liu and her colleagues observed that Christianity in Hong Kong was a middle-class movement, that working-class people were essentially unreached. The project began with extensive research of working-class culture; Dr. Liu worked for months as a seamstress in a factory to learn working-class culture, dialect, vocabulary, values, needs, heroes and heroines. She became intimately familiar with the monotony, futility, alienation, and work-induced sicknesses experienced by these people.

Liu and her colleagues started lay-led "factory fellowships" within the factories. As factory workers became Christians, Liu and her colleagues interviewed them, gathered data, and developed a model of how Chinese secular working populations become Christians. Dr. Liu's model departs from the conventional evangelical wisdom summarized in the "Engel Scale," because the interview data forced the reluctant conclusion that the essence of conversion for this population was *not* the transfer of theological beliefs, especially in the early phases of conversion. The resulting "Liu Scale" is a triangle—whose three sides are *Attitudes*, *Experiences*, and, at the base but coming last in the life history of converts, *Theological Knowledge*.

Conversion among secular Chinese working-class people in Hong Kong typically begins with four attitude changes. Once, they found church "boring," and they could not identify with "Christians." Their pilgrimage typically begins when they relate to and identify with some Christians that they like and enjoy. Next, they begin to like church (worship services) and to think of church as okay. Next, they start "liking Jesus," and they become open to learning more about him. Then, in time, they become open to commitment to Jesus.

Somewhere near, or past, the middle of this sequence of attitude changes, a series of pivotal experiences enters their life history. First, most of these converts typically have one or more experiences of answered prayer. Indeed, those who witness will encourage these people to experiment with faith and to pray to the Lord about their needs, and so they pray about their life concerns—such as their hope to pass a driver's license test. Second, many of them experience the power of Jesus—as in the healing of a sickness, or the casting out of a demon, or the discovered power for positive self-esteem. Third, they experience Jesus as the Lord who forgives, saves from sin, and leads them in a new life.

Somewhere near, or past, the middle of this sequence of experiences, they become open to Scripture and theological knowledge. They had been exposed to such data before, but were not very attentive; they were more conscious of the friendship or love they were experiencing in the church. Now, they start appropriating ideas they were exposed to before, and now they typically hunger to know more, to study the Scriptures.

Impressive church growth and creative outreach are now occurring in Hong Kong, as informed by this model. There are over one hundred factory fellowships, and more than a dozen working-class congregations. The work has spread to reach restaurant workers, taxi drivers, prostitutes, drug addicts, and Tamil Indian immigrants. Congregations for restaurant workers and their families now worship Sunday evenings at 9:00 P.M., because that is when they get off work; for the same reason, congregations for taxi drivers and their families now gather at midnight.

A congregation for addicts meets in the open air under trees, where one can observe some indigenous symbols for their new faith. From the tree at the front, recovering drug addicts have hung their needles, alcoholics their bottles, and gamblers their racing tickets. This very public service, with an indigenous liturgy using symbols that relate to the congregation's life struggles, now attracts others into faith.

3. The "Target" model

From my interviews with converts from secularity, and my studies of churches reaching them, it is now possible to present another distinct version of the steps that many secular people take toward deep faith. Imagine a four-ringed target for throwing darts; and imagine secular people as beyond the outer circle, having missed the target for which God aimed their lives (Romans 3:23). The "bull's eye" represents God's goal for us. That is, God calls each person to become the kind of disciple living in faith, hope, and love, and for the will of God, that the New Testament describes and the christian movement needs. Each step toward the "bull's eye" involves responding to God's grace by crossing a "barrier" (represented below as A, B, C, and D).

A. *The Image Barrier*: Secular people who are "farthest away" typically begin with their backs (or sides) toward the faith because of a negative "image" of Christianity.

One version of the image barrier, held by people still scripted by enlightenment ideas, assumes that Christianity is "untrue." These people still believe in a machine-like universe, they still bet on human reason to deliver ultimate truth and a consensus morality, they still count on science and education to save the world. With an enlightenment worldview, they assume that Christianity is "disproved'' or is ''the same'' as other religions. But, as the dust continues to settle and increasing numbers lose confidence in the enlightenment alternative, more people will be open to other faith options—including Christianity. Churches can accelerate the dismantling of modernity by exposing and puncturing the remaining enlightenment balloons, and by offering the christian alternative as they communicate christian truth claims on secular turf, in secular language, with the support of good reasons.

A second ''image problem'' with Christianity involves the assumption that Christianity is ''irrelevant'' to their lives and/or to community and world concerns. (Many of them once had experience in an irrelevant church, and generalized to all churches from that experience.) Many churches can (and do) challenge that image by becoming more ''relevant'' than any other fellowship or institution, by joining people and communities in their struggles, and by communicating the relevance of real Christianity to people's needs. Secular people bridge this barrier when they discover a church that is, in fact, relevant, and they become ''seekers.''

A third image problem with Christianity involves the assumption that Christianity is ''boring.'' These people, raised on television sit coms in an entertainment age, find ''church'' to be insufficiently interesting or stimulating. In response, some churches have discovered that ''it is okay to make it interesting,'' and they develop approaches, liturgy, and discourse that adapt to short attention spans and stimulate, and even amuse, while teaching and inspiring.[20]

B. *The Culture Barrier*: Once a person becomes a seeker, the second barrier the secular seeker typically experiences is a cultural barrier—or the ''stained-glass barrier.'' When secular people do visit a church, it can be a culturally alienating experience. If they do not understand the jargon, relate to the music, identify with the people, or feel comfortable in the facility, they infer that Christianity (and the christian God) is not for people like them. This cultural barrier is not usually perceived by the church, especially when the target population represents the same general culture as the church membership; the church assumes that ''they'' do understand and relate to what we do, or they ''should.'' But secular people who aren't already ''churchbroke'' usually experience us as a different subculture from them, and as more culturally distant from them than we think they ''should.'' This cultural barrier is sometimes crossed when an earnest seeker agrees to "become circumcised"; they submit to reinculturation and become like "church people." That happens often enough to seduce churches into thinking there is no cultural barrier, or that all seekers should be eager to adapt to our ways. But the churches that reach much greater numbers of secular people pay the price to become much more indigenous to the people in their mission field, thus removing the cultural barrier that prevents, for now, most people from considering the faith itself.

C. *The Gospel Barrier*: Once the image and cultural barriers are crossed or removed, seekers are free to consider the gospel itself—the only stumbling block that people should face.[21] There are several dominant paradigms (covenant, kingdom, justification, atonement, forgiveness, reconciliation, salvation) in the biblical gospel—presumably because no one paradigm conveys the full reality of God's deed in Jesus Christ—and there are many cultural forms for communicating the meaning within each paradigm. Probably the most widely used, and useful, single expression is the credo of the New Life for All Movement in Africa and Latin America:

1. God created all people for Life.
2. People, in their sin, have forfeited Life.
3. God came in Christ to offer people New Life.
4. People can receive this New Life by Turning
   from their sins
   to Christ in trust and obedience
   to the Community of New Life.
5. People knowing New Life are called to be faithful in all relationships.

Many denominations, traditions, and movements use some version of the New Life for All approach because (a) It begins with creation—as the Bible does. (b) It includes the Church as part of God's saving provision. (c) It includes the christian ethic and life-style as part of the message. (d) It begins with people's life concerns—a nearly universal point of contact. (e) Any christian theological tradition can use it, and presumably in most any culture.

Most churches reaching secular people distill some such cogent version(s) of the gospel, because seekers often experience the gospel barrier as an intimidating thicket of more theological trees, bushes, limbs, and vines than they can grope through. Effective churches help seekers with this theological barrier in several ways. First, the churches focus on the faith's foundational truth claims, and do not, for now, try to teach everything. For example, a church may discern that certain convictions about God, Jesus, sin, reconciliation, the love ethic, and the Kingdom of God are essential to producing real disciples, while convictions about angels, consubstantiation, Jonah's whale, and the date Ephesians was written are less essential. Once people become Christians, in time they can affirm many things they could not have affirmed at their time of entry. Second, the churches help with the theological barrier by meaningfully interpreting the foundational convictions of Christianity, rather than merely perpetuating and parroting the tradition. Third, they join seekers in the discovery of the good reasons that support many christian truth claims. Fourth, they encourage an experiment of faith, that people may experience the validity of Christianity as a threshold to commitment. Fifth, they give people time, and they nurture the adoption process, while encouraging closure in measurable time.

D. *The Total Commitment Barrier:* Once people accept the gospel and are Christians, the fourth barrier or challenge relates to becoming a totally committed Christian who seeks and obeys God's will and lives to advance God's Kingdom. When people first become Christians, typically they do so for Christ's benefits. They want (and receive) meaning for their lives, or higher self-esteem, or glue for their marriage, or the experience of acceptance, or the promise of heaven. But, as the evangelical tradition has often expressed it, they have received Jesus as Savior, but not yet as Lord. If they fail to become totally devoted, they become nominal Christians—almost as selfish and self-seeking as they were before, never experiencing the transforming power that Christianity promises, and not embodying the authenticity that seekers look for to see if Christianity delivers on its promises. So, effective churches invite and challenge their Christians, for their sakes and the world's sake, to a life of obedience to the will of God.[22]

This ultimate evangelical challenge is so formidable that some churches dodge it and appear content to have people (depending on the tradition) "saved" or "confirmed." We noted earlier that secular people do not know that the God of the Bible is their Lord, that their rightful response to the Lord is lifetime commitment to God's will.

Frequently, people who have moved past the image, cultural, and gospel barriers are as unaware as rank pagans of God's radical claim upon His people. Bill Hybels, and everyone else who commends this full gospel, reports that "becoming totally devoted to Christ" is the most difficult single topic to get across to people. "When I teach that to secularly minded people, they think I'm from Mars. The thought of living according to someone else's agenda is ludicrous; it contradicts Western culture's myth that 'you can have it all.' "[23]

4. The "Multiple Conversations" model

Traditional evangelism is famous (or infamous) for trying to engineer decisions to become Christian in one (confrontational) conversation. By contrast, we are observing that a "Multiple Conversations" model is more promising for reaching many secular people than traditional evangelism's "single confrontation" model, especially for people already turned off and alienated by earlier confrontation experiences.

Yet, the differences between the two models should not be exaggerated, because "soft" confrontation is necessary at key times during conversations. Asking questions is one form of soft confrontation. For example, Robert Schuller often asks newly involved people "Why does a good intelligent person like you not embrace the christian faith?" Their response usually surfaces barriers to discipleship—which can then be explored. Bruce Larson once learned, from a physician, the value of three questions in helping open people to the gospel: "Do you ever ask yourself what you are getting out of life?" "Do you ever ask yourself the meaning of life?" "Do you have a sense of dread or foreboding, panic or terror?"[24]

Canon Bryan Green's ministry to the city of Birmingham, England, included a Thursday evening group for "sixth formers," that is, intelligent, pre-university youth aged 16 to 18. The group was composed of youth who were not yet believers, with questions and doubts, who were willing to discuss, ask questions, "experiment" with the christian faith, and be "open" to the group's conversation and to God's spirit. Typically, a visiting speaker would briefly present an idea, and the remainder of the hour and a half was spent in questions, challenges, mutual probing. When I was the visiting speaker on several occasions, I observed that Canon Green functioned as a member of the group, occasionally saying something, more often observing the faces and body language of group members. I often sensed he was praying for them. During the refreshment time, Green would engage in brief personal conversation with one or more persons who had revealed some receptivity or special struggle in the session. He would ask questions like "What is Jesus beginning to mean to you?" "What do you find you are almost believing?" "How much more time do you need to decide about following Christ?" Green never pressured anyone, nor would he acquiesce to the illusion that one can take forever to decide these matters. His role was to facilitate a response to Christ, yea or nay, in measurable time—usually several months.

The other form of soft confrontation involves multiple conversations that usually begin with the seeker's agenda. A businessman visited for months the First Church of Christ in Wethersfield, Connecticut, and then he stopped coming. Donald Morgan approached him at his business, and asked, "Ron, how is your faith?"

The man replied, "I don't know. I have a lot of questions."

"Well, let's talk a few times," Morgan suggested. "Let's get your questions out." After a half dozen visits, Morgan asked, "Want to come in again?"

"No," the man replied. "That's it. I have worked it out. I want to confess faith and join the church." He has been an active devoted layman ever since.

Kenneth Chafin often invites people to conversation as a form of pulpit invitation: "There are some of you who are struggling with the decision to become a Christian, but you need conversation. You don't need to walk down the aisle, but you do need conversation. Why don't you invite me to your office, or your home, or come to my office by appointment?" Often, at Walnut Street Baptist Church, people become Christians by this kind of sequence: A person watches the Walnut Street services on television for some months, then attends worship services and becomes involved in a Sunday school class. In time, the class teacher will make a referral: "Ken, Tony comes out of a Roman Catholic background. Something is happening in his life, and Christianity is now becoming real to him. If he called, could he come by and see you?" Tony then takes the initiative (which is psychologically important) and Chafin and Tony have several conversations over time. At some point, Chafin shares the gospel, relates it to Tony's struggle, invites Tony in principle to receive Christ and become a disciple, and then adds, with no pressure to decide now: "Please let me know when you are ready." Then, in some later conversation, the person signals that he is ready. "At this point, they have already made their decision; they are asking for help in processing it."

Willow Creek Community Church coaches its army of laypeople to engage in a very similar ministry of evangelical conversation. Once they have established a credible relationship with an unchurched seeker, they pray that the Holy Spirit will open up an opportunity to share the gospel. When they share the gospel, they do *not* expect, or invite, an immediate response. Bill Hybels explains that if someone did accept the gospel in four minutes, "we would wonder about their emotional stability, or if they really understood!" Rather, the shared gospel plants a seed, which starts them thinking and asking questions—which become the agenda for a series of conversations over weeks, or even months, before the seeker reaches closure.

THE THEOLOGY WE COMMUNICATE

As we ask "*What* communicates with secular people?" seven suggestions are warranted regarding the Christian theology we communicate, and how we effectively communicate it.

1. The theology that reaches secular people will most likely be consistent with "the faith delivered to the saints," what Tom Oden calls "Classical Christianity"—as distilled in the early Christian creeds. When secular people move toward Christianity, they usually want "the real thing"—and not some "new theology." This means that some churches, as once in Luther's Germany and Wesley's England, will need to recover Classical Christianity. In *The Everlasting Man*, G. K. Chesterton reminds us that "again and again, before our time, men have grown content with a diluted doctrine. And again and again there has followed on that dilution, coming as out of the darkness in a crimson cataract, the strength of the red original wine."

New theologies—whether liberal, neo-orthodox, process, or liberation—do serve important functions in the Church. They enable us to retain some people in the household of faith who lose confidence in the prevailing orthodoxy, and new theologies contribute to innovation within the tradition. But new theologies are virtually impotent for making new Christians from the world; the secular people who want something new opt for a new religion. In particular, the more liberal theologies that bought the Enlightenment's teachings about the goodness of humanity, an underlying affinity between all religions, and the Enlightenment's anti-supernaturalism bias, have failed to engage the very "modern mind" for which they were accommodating.

2. The truth claims of classical Christianity are not effectively communicated merely by parroting the tradition. The claims must be meaningfully interpreted to the culture and life situations of the given secular population, and this often involves patient explanation in the language of ordinary human experience. Unfortunately, as Alan Walker notes, "An idolatry of words has grown up in evangelism. There are many people who, if they fail to hear the repetition of phrases and words with which they are familiar, make the sometimes absurd claim that the gospel is not being preached."[25] The Church's problem with an idolatry of the word is not confined to the evangelical party. Several other parties also work to engineer linguistic conformity, as witnessed in the movement to enforce language that is politically correct.

We have surfaced the one tension producer from which no Christian communicator to secular people will ever be totally free. Your language will never "please all of the people all of the time." The language that appeals to some group in the church will miss the outsiders; the language that engages the person with no Christian memory won't sound sufficiently religious, or evangelical, or inclusive, or traditional, or avant garde, or yuppie to some insiders. How does the apostle resolve this dilemma? By speaking for and to the unchurched, while patiently explaining to the faithful, over and over again, what one is doing as a communicator, and why, and encouraging them to do likewise! Every Christian who decides for apostolic ministry will discover the need for this communication policy. Alan Walker discovered this need as a young communicator. After he preached at a church, a secular visitor asked for his sermon manuscript. Several days later

he returned the manuscript with each phrase underlined which he did not understand. There were about forty such words and phrases. He wanted to know, for example, what "in Christ" meant. . . . It brought home to me a lesson I have never forgotten. I believe any Christian who would dare to declare his faith to another must escape from the jargon of his own discipline of thought and make his gospel intelligible by the use of relevant, freshly minted expressions of truth.[26]

What is it about the Church's traditional language that prevents secular people from understanding what we mean? Sometimes the problem is with a word's *denotation*. The mind may have no referent at all for "propitiation" or "sanctification"; or the mind may assign a wrong referent, as when one connects "Kingdom" to King Arthur or Henry VIII. Sometimes the problem is with a word's *connotation* in the mind, from earlier experiences or conditioning. So, for secular people "sin" may connote sex, and "redemption" may connote green stamps.

What might reminting the language look like? *The Good News Bible* provides a good model for expressing the biblical message in the English vernacular. Often, the effective communicator employs the most accurate available synonym that the target population understands. Paul Tillich substituted "acceptance" for "justification." Lord Soper speaks of Christ "rescuing" people rather than "saving" them. Rick Warren finds that "Lord" is not indigenous to Southern California, and may refer to Jesus as "manager" or "CEO." Not many secular people are familiar with "demons" that possess and destroy people; but they are familiar with the legion of "addictions" that possess and destroy people! Jim Harnish interprets Paul's doctrine of justification in terms of the "work addiction" that drives many people, himself included.

Paul discovered what we need to discover: we are saved, made valuable, given worth because we are loved by God, "not because of works." . . . The universe, even the immediate universe that seems to swirl around me, is ultimately not dependent upon me. . . . As I look at my own life and the community in which I live, I sometimes wonder if the most common, most insidious heresy of our times is our desire to find the meaning of our life, the justification of our existence in the work of our hands.[27]

Language, however, is only one of the components in the total complex process of interpreting the gospel. It may not be the most important component. A "stained-glass voice" or a ministerial tone can poison the communication process even more than unclear word choice, so effective advocates communicate with culturally appropriate naturalness. The ethos, or credibility, of the communicator(s) is probably more important. Since "no one can say 'Jesus is Lord' except by the Holy Spirit," the Spirit's role in evangelization is more important. But culturally appropriate language that is accurate, clear, and preferably interesting to the target population is a prerequisite to effective communication; there is little effective communication without it.

3. Many secular people are turned off by "dogma," and therefore may not now be open to parts of the biblical canon, such as the Old Testament or books by John and Paul, that they associate with dogma. But many are interested in Jesus and what Jesus had to say. When George Gallup's pollsters asked Americans which historical figure they would most like to spend a day with, nearly two out of three chose Jesus—including 37 percent of the people who claimed no church affiliation.[28] So the christian strategist may have to witness, with some people, out of a functionally reduced canon—the Synoptic Gospels.

4. When communicating with secular people, we may explore a new sequence of possibilities. For example, we may need to begin with Jesus' humanity rather than his divinity, which would let this person find Christ in the same sequence of discoveries that the earliest disciples experienced. As William Temple used to say, "If we introduce Jesus to people in His full humanity, the divinity will take care of itself."

Likewise, Bruce Larson suggests that when we explain Christianity's trinitarian understanding of God, the usual sequence of "Father, Son, and Holy Spirit" reverses the New Testament strategy in approaching people.

We come to people first of all with the doctrine of God the Father, which is the most difficult of the Christian doctrines to comprehend. We then talk about the doctrine of the Son, which is more understandable, and finally, we save the Holy Spirit for those inside in church who are most mature. . . . We should begin with the Holy Spirit himself. The outsider can understand the Spirit of God loose in people. . . . As people respond to the warmth of the Spirit in other people, they can then be taught about the Son, and finally, as they mature, grapple with the doctrine of God the Father.[29]

Again, while the usual sequence in becoming a Christian is repentance, then commitment, some cases require the opposite sequence. Larson recalls:

Once a man drove two hundred miles to see me for the express purpose of giving his life to Christ. For two hours we sat in my study while I asked him to tell me the things in his life that needed changing, but he kept insisting, "I can't think of a thing."
I probed and probed until I almost killed the patient. Finally I asked, "Well, why don't we get on with the business of commitment?" "That's what I came for," he replied. As we knelt together, this man made a stumbling but genuine surrender—and *then* for the next half hour he poured out the habits, fears, sins, and wrong relationships of a lifetime.[30]

The christian communicator who is open to God, and open to beginning where people are, will thus discover that the unchaining of his or her own imagination is indispensable to reaching secular people.

5. The Kingdom of God is a message needing meaningful interpretation in our post-enlightenment West. The Kingdom message involves the good news that history is not out of control, but that God is in control, and that God's purposes will prevail. We have the opportunity to reintroduce purpose to a secular world that, because of science's conditioning, is preoccupied with cause and effect and blind to the issues of purpose for human life and history. The gospel of the Kingdom of God proclaims that, in Jesus' teaching and ministry, God has revealed the goals of history, has launched in the Church's mission a movement to work for those goals, and has challenged us to join this movement and make a difference. For example, Jim Harnish recalls:

A twenty-six-year-old Englishwoman in 1846 was struggling in her conscience with what God would have her do with her life. She recorded this prayer, "O God, Thou puttest into my heart this great desire to devote myself to the sick and sorrowful." Later she prayed, "Give me my work to do."

God gave her work to do, but who would have ever predicted that Florence Nightingale's work in the filthy hospital barracks of the Crimean War would transform everything that we understand of hospital and nursing care? She simply did what she believed God had called her to do.[31]

6. The relevant communication of the gospel to secular people will emphasize the doctrine of vocation (that every person has a "calling") and the meaning of work. Donald Morgan observed that, even though American society was built in part on the Puritan work ethic—because the Puritans saw clearly the relationship between faith and work, the church today usually ignores the world of work—perhaps reflecting a bias in some theologians that business people are the enemy and the have-nots are the real people of God (more likely because of the prejudice that it is unholy to be successful or to make money). Dorothy Sayers is said to have observed that

In nothing has the church so lost her hold on reality as in her failure to understand and respect the secular vocation. She has allowed work and religion to become separate departments, and is astonished to find that, as a result, the secular work of the world is turned to purely selfish and destructive ends, become irreligious, or at least, uninterested in religion. But is this astonishing? How can anyone remain interested in a religion which seems to have no concern with nine-tenths of his life?

Samuel Shoemaker challenged this gap between Sunday religion and the weekday world of work, which tragically suggested that God is interested in "religion" but not in life—a flagrant denial of the Incarnation. He launched, through Calvary Episcopal Church, Pittsburgh, "The Pittsburgh Experiment"—to apply the christian vision and spirit to the business world of the city. He proclaimed: "As Christians, we are not called to leave behind us the body, money, work, amusements, statecraft: we are called upon to redeem these things by using them for God. . . . There is nothing more 'spiritual' or holy about going to church than about going to the office, if you go to both places to serve and obey God." The Experiment involved (a) converting some men and women in business who will then take Christ's Spirit into the workplace, (b) a christian approach to human relations in the work setting, (c) meeting and yoking with colleagues who share the commitment, (d) adding the service motive to business practice, thereby putting the "profit" quest in proper perspective, (e) working for the integrity of products and services, and (f) working for practical justice in business organizations. He collected, told, and published the stories of disciples who were working out their vocation in corporations and institutions, believing them to be fully as heroic and faithful as believers who follow Christ to "the swamps of Africa." He discovered that when Christianity's redemptive relevance to business and work is proclaimed, many people are attracted.[32]

7. One special objective for reaching secular people is to communicate an accurate and positive "image" of Christianity. Russell Hale observed, in his interviews with unchurched Americans, that most unchurched people have never heard good news from the church, but only bad news. What they have heard "is overloaded with law, moralism, judgement, and rejection—a legalistic rulebook morality in Christian clothing." He adds that "many have simply never heard of a loving God who accepts people while they are yet sinners."[33]

Robert Schuller identifies other images of Christianity that merit the Christian's strategic response. Secular people who believe, with Ted Turner, that "Christianity is a religion for losers" need to see some Christians as "winners" and achievers, with Christianity making other people winners—on Christianity's terms. Secular people who equate Christianity with superstition—on a level with black cats and ladders—need to see that Christianity makes sense. Secular people who see Christianity as anti-intellectual or anti-education need to know intelligent and educated Christians. Secular people who see Christianity as unscientific or anti-science need to know that, historically, Christianity's teaching that the creation is not divine liberated the human mind for scientific investigation, and that many Christians contribute to science and profit from science; but the Church will also serve this generation by exposing the limits of the scientific worldview and thereby free people from the idolatry of science. Secular people who image Christians as critical, unkind, unloving people need to meet nonjudgmental, affirming, kind, and loving Christians. Secular people who image Christians as phoney or hypocritical need to meet authentic and consistent Christians.

COMMUNICATION APPROACHES TO SECULAR PEOPLE

Finally, what specific communication approaches are known to be effective with secular people? Before addressing that question, consider some approaches that are *not* effective. Donald Morgan's church in New England receives many people who were turned off elsewhere, and they tell their "war stories." When I asked Donald Morgan, "What are the biggest mistakes Christians make in trying to reach unchurched people?" he drew from their negative experiences:

Would-be evangelists alienate people when they put them down, or talk down to them, or reveal, perhaps in body language, that they don't respect them. We turn them off when we don't take the time to find out where they are coming from, or when we act as though we have all the answers. Perhaps most of all, we miss engaging people when we fail to perceive and appreciate the faith they already have, and the hunger for faith they have.

To avoid the mistakes that Donald Morgan has observed, I feature ten specific, positive things that effective communicators *do* to assist God's revelation.

1. The first, and as important as any, is "active listening." Russell Hale counsels us to discover the other person's "sufferings, hostility, and alienation—even with the confession that the evangelist has been there too." It is important that they experience our acceptance, our interest in them, even our liking them. Hale stresses that many people outside the church want, and need, to be heard. They all have a story that includes some negative experiences; when they share that story, and their meaning and feelings are understood, they may be more ready to hear and to consider change. Hale declares:

Readiness to hear or learn is the absolute precondition for change. Prior to any readiness to hear the good news . . . is the necessity of the outsider's letting out those feelings that prevent a hearing of that message. Listening—honest, perceptive, nonjudgemental, relational—which conveys trust and acceptance of the other, is the requisite element in the communication process. People can't hear until they have been heard.[34]

2. Many effective communicators first engage people on neutral turf, or their turf, in the secular world and not in the church building—a principle dramatized in John Wesley's field preaching; in Donald Soper's open-air speaking, Labour Party meetings, and the House of Lords; in Agnes Liu's factory fellowships; in Alan Walker's Sunday Evening people's service in a theater in downtown Sydney; in Samuel Shoemaker's "interviews" in homes, offices, and alleys; in Robert Schuller's television ministry; in Billy Graham's crusade services in a football stadium. Many secular people become less receptive on ecclesiastical turf, and many will not walk through the doors of a church. Effective modern apostles know that the world of neighborhoods, schools, factories, offices, institutions, media, and "systems" defines the marketplace of ideas and life options in which Christianity must become consciously competitive. David Womack contends that "the apostolic seed" was never meant to be confined to hothouses, receiving sunlight only through stained-glass windows, walled off from the outside world, "where it cannot compete in the open environment of the earth." . . . What is the answer?

The plant must break out of its stained-glass sanctuary and take its life into the open fields. Its seeds must be scattered on the soil of every nation. It must be nurtured, encouraged, turned loose in its wild, uncontrollable state. It must be freed to the force of the wind and the driving of the rain, for the seed carries in its cells the knowledge of its own destiny. It must take root and bear fruit in every conceivable environment on the face of the planet.[35]

3. An effective communicator relates to seekers as a friend and ally, not an adversary who is out to "win" them. They function as "consultants" who are helping people to find faith, not as hard sell persuaders who are talking them into believing or joining. And, knowing that seeking people have contradictory forces within them—some forces driving them toward faith, and some away from faith—effective communicators relate to the part of them that wants faith. They relate to them out of positive assumptions about them rather than negative assumptions. They relate to them as persons who *want* to be Christians but who have not yet found the door.

4. Effective communicators do not try to do all the communicating. They know that the faith is "more caught than taught," that a person's meaningful "involvement" can do its own communicating,

and that involvement helps people discover the faith for themselves; so they get seekers involved in the fellowship, message, and service of the congregations. Many people come to believe from several months of involvement.

Jim Harnish observes that, for most people, faith is discovered in the opposite pattern to evangelical assumptions: "I grew up thinking that the sequence was accept Jesus, then read the Bible, then get into fellowship and service in the world. But I learned that, usually, it is just the opposite; they get involved first, then they ask the biblical and theological questions, and then they move into commitment." Often, Harnish does not even ask new people if they believe in Jesus Christ; he just "gets them involved" in group life, worship, scripture study, prayer, service, and conversation.

5. Effective communicators speak early to the questions, unmet needs, and unfulfilled motives that drive secular people's lives. Secular people continue in their assumption that Christianity is not "relevant" to their lives until we correlate the facet of the gospel that is good news for their felt need. The "point of contact" between Christianity and people is the point at which some facet of the gospel engages a pressing human need. Informed apostles are very clear about what needs they intend to engage in their audiences. So, for instance, Bryan Green delineates the following human needs as providing ready points of contact:

A general sense of neediness, loneliness, a fear, lack of purpose, shame, powerlessness to overcome a habit, inability to meet life's demands, a sense of frustration, desire for truth, desire for immortality, desire to help others but no power to do it, suffering, moral failure, weakness of will, frustration over evil in the world.[36]

Every apostle I interviewed has an easily recalled catalogue of human needs that provide points of contact for the christian good news. Donald Morgan fluently recalled a litany of such needs: How to deal with failure, disappointment, and success; "They are almost as afraid of success as of failure!" How to discover meaning and purpose for life. How to gain the power to live the life you want to live. How to build meaningful relationships, and how to cope with loneliness. How to get faith, and how to get peace of mind. "How to have a relationship with God, despite everything." How to live the christian life and be involved in the world, and how to "square your faith with the business world." How can Christianity make me a better parent and spouse? Morgan believes that part of the answer to many needs and questions is the larger perspective that faith provides. He shares the following story:

> So live with an eternal view. When you have it, you're less likely to fret and fidget. You're more likely to be at peace, to be serene and tranquil. It's like the widow in Vermont who lost her home by fire. Her neighbors decided to band together and build her a house, and so asked her what changes she would like in her new home which was to be modeled after the old one. She thought about this for awhile, and then she said, "I'll tell you what—I'd just love to have a window over my kitchen sink."
> There you have it! . . . Live with an eternal view! Have a window over your kitchen sink![37]

One need that will not go away relates to the perennial problem of suffering, that is, "Why do good people suffer?" As his constituents experience tragedy, or suffering, or the death of a child, Jim Harnish reports that he spends more time with more people around this struggle than any other. The "folk theology" of American civil religion says "God must have a reason for this crap." Harnish spends much of his life explaining that "God did not cause this" and "there is no escape or quick fix," and proclaiming that "God suffers with us and gives us the grace we need."[38]

In many of their needs, of course, secular people of the West are not unique; they are driven by many of the same needs and fears of the entire human race. Albert Schweitzer once commented on his approach to preaching in Africa: "Oh, these people are born scared, live scared, and die scared. I limit myself to preaching to them that in spite of all appearances to the contrary, behind all the seeming mystery and cruelty of life, there is not terror but love, the Father of Jesus Christ."[39] Substitute "anxiety" for "fear," and that same message preaches anywhere in the West.

But often the particular form of the need or question varies from one culture to another. For example, Alan Walker observes three forms in which the issue of "God" is expressed. In Australia and much of Europe, the existence of God is an issue, so the apostle must present "an apologetic for God." In the United States, the issue is not the existence of God but "what kind of God? Is it the God of American civil religion or the Father of Jesus Christ?" and so the apostle proclaims the kind of God we find in Christ and Scripture. In much of the Two-Thirds World, the issue is evil spirits, so the apostle presents Jesus Christ as *Christus Victor*—the Savior from fear.

By relating to seeking secular people at the points of their needs, even when those needs are self-centered, evangelizers thereby fulfill the cardinal rule of effective evangelism—that "we begin where people are, rather than where we would like them to be." Perhaps our most frequent mistake in evangelism is to begin where we are, with our interests, rather than where they are; this sometimes takes the form, in Jim Harnish's words, of "dumping some theological baggage before it is asked for." We can begin where they are—even their self-interest—trusting that, in God's good time, their involvement with the christian message, fellowship, and service will draw them out of mere self-interest into a new life, new relationships, and new life-style.

However, actually finding where a given person is open presents something of a challenge. Bruce Larson builds on Harry Emerson Fosdick's insight that—if every man is like an island, then we must "row around him" until we find a suitable place to land. "Each man has a landing place where we can make contact with him and establish a beachhead for what God ultimately intends."[40]

Regardless of the particular need we identify, there is one underlying need in every secular seeker, and one thing that must happen before they can become Christians. The penultimate goal of every evangelist should be, in Ken Chafin's words:

the breakdown of this feeling that "I can run my own life." Whether that comes from failure, or from empty success, that has to take place. That is the secular equivalent to admitting that you are a sinner. . . . It may come with a sense of purposelessness; it may come in many ways. But a person has to realize and own the fact that "I'm not managing my life well. Life isn't going well. This is not what I think life should be, life should be more than this." That sense of need has to be there.

Chafin has observed enough people long enough to believe that time works for the patient christian advocate. "I have noticed that when you are in contact with people and constantly exposing them to the gospel, something happens in their life that opens their hearing up. I now live with the assurance that the events of life's realities will have a way, ultimately, of cracking that veneer of indifference. So I will get a shot at them, and I know I will get a shot at them!''

Bill Hybels lives with this same assurance, and recommends an intervention now that increases our chances of reaching them later: "Offer your help for a later date.''[41] Many secular people get their act together for a season and experience no conscious needs—a state that Donald Soper called "temporary euphoria.'' Hybels' experience concludes that "to people who are that self-deceived, there's nothing I can say. It does no good to try to convince them of their need. But publicly or privately I can offer my assistance for the day they finally realize they need Christ.''[42] In the years Hybels served as chaplain of the Chicago Bears, he made that offer to players while they were on a roll—and several responded later, when their bubble burst.

Once people do own their need and confess that they cannot manage their life, Ken Chafin is clear that the invitation to respond to Christ must be defined in terms of the surrender and commitment of one's life to Christ. He believes that the "clever little definitions of faith that do not involve life commitment are unbiblical,'' and they prevent people from experiencing the profound life change and fulfillment that comes only through giving one's life to the God who gave himself for us. Furthermore, life commitment "needs to find its expression in the community of believers.''

6. Effective communicators are aware that the communication of the christian message's meaning takes place, by cumulative effect, over time, so they nourish the adoption process over time. As one expression of this principle, the effective communicator takes seriously the fact that the christian movement is entrusted with a multifaceted gospel—good news of the love of God, the grace of God, the Kingdom of God, forgiveness of sins, reconciliation, new birth, justification, and sanctification. The communicator should not attempt to communicate every jewel in the gospel treasure in one transaction, because such would submit people to "information overload"—which repels people, or induces superficial acceptance. The communicator feels free to present one facet of the gospel at a time—usually beginning with the facet most relevant to the seeker's felt need.

7. Effective communicators "personalize" the message. They consciously try to speak to individuals, even if formally addressing a large audience, because response cannot begin until a person understands that the gospel is "for me," or at least "for people like me." The historian of American revivalism, William Warren Sweet, was perhaps the first scholar to see the connection between personalizing and response: "To personalize religion is to emotionalize it."[43] By helping people to identify with the message we can engage them with appropriate intensity and facilitate their response, without indulging in the conspicuous "emotional appeals" for which evangelism has often been criticized. Canon Green concludes that "each person matters. [In] an audience of thousands . . . I must be on the lookout for that individual to whom God is speaking. . . . *There is no such thing as mass evangelism*. We can preach to people in the mass, but each soul must be won for Christ individually."[44]

8. Effective communicators do not "put the pressure on" for people to respond. Many secular people are already too pressured and driven to exercise good judgment, so the caring communicator may take pressure off and increase their comfort. Jim Harnish observes that people do not want to be pressured, pushed, or rushed. So, "my task is to create lots of options for people to respond, and let them know there is no one way." When Harnish visits receptive people in their home, he typically raises the need to decide to follow Christ and join Christ's Body, and then says, "I am ready when you are. We won't pressure you, but we sure do want you."

9. Many christian communicators will find communication value in word plays, proverbs, and other maxims that distill important truths in a vivid form that people can recall for reflection. (Aristotle saw that maxims invest speech with a sense of proven wisdom.) The Hebrew prophets used word play and proverb repeatedly. And Jesus employed this device—as in the Golden Rule. Proverbial statements are undervalued by elitist scholars as bumper-sticker theology, but most people hear and recall them gladly. Robert Schuller has effectively rediscovered this device; I meet many people who are engaged by proverbs or word plays that they first heard or read from him; for example, "When the going gets tough, the tough get

going.'' ''If it's going to be it's up to me.'' ''Turn your scars into stars.'' ''Inch by inch, anything is a cinch.'' ''Tough times never last, but tough people do.'' ''Build a dream and the dream will build you.'' ''Believe in the God who believes in you.'' ''God's delays are not God's denials.'' ''Find a need and fill it, find a hurt and heal it.'' ''What you are is God's gift to you. What you make of yourself is your gift to God.''

10. Many effective christian communicators have recovered the art of discovering and telling stories, particularly ''redemptive analogies,'' and the kinds of stories that enable people to more or less discover the point for themselves. Bill Hybels observed that secular seekers resist the biblical instruction, ''Don't be unequally yoked,'' as discriminatory; ''Why should I refuse to marry someone I love simply because her religion is a little different?'' Hybel's analogy explains ''why I think God would write such an outrageous prescription'':

What if I went out to [our church's] construction site, and I found one contractor, with his fifteen workers, busily constructing our building from one set of plans, and then I went to another side of the building, and here's another contractor building his part of the building from a totally different set of blueprints? There'd be total chaos.

Friends . . . what happens in a marriage when you've got a husband who says ''I'm going to build this marriage on this blueprint,'' and a wife who says, ''I'm going to build it on *this* blueprint?'' They collide, and usually the strongest person wins—for a time. But then there's destruction.

God wants his children to build solid, permanent relationships, and he knows it's going to take a single set of plans. In order to build a solid building or a sound marriage, you need one set of blueprints.[45]

Another story, from the legacy of Alfred North Whitehead, the celebrated Harvard philosopher, helps us understand the depth of the christian message for those secular people who are seeking and questioning.

One day, Whitehead lectured on cosmology. A sophomore student confronted Whitehead in his office after the lecture, saying, ''You've got it all wrong.'' Whitehead, wondering where the fellow was coming from, asked, ''What is your understanding of the structure of the universe?''

The student replied, with great confidence, "The whole universe sits on the back of a turtle."

Whitehead, hesitant to condescend toward a student, asked, "What is the turtle standing on?"

The student quickly answered, "On the back of another turtle."

Whitehead was asking what *that* turtle stood on when the student interrupted, saying, "Look, I know what you are going to ask next, so let me answer: It's turtles all the way down!"

The eccentric student was raising the ultimate question: What is it that "goes all the way down"?

The christian movement represents the creative, accepting, empowering compassion that goes all the way down. We Christians represent the ultimate reality, revealed in Jesus Christ, for whom all people search. We are entrusted with this great news for all humanity. We are called, in this generation, to mount a great movement for the reevangelization of the West.

What Kind of Christians Reach Secular People?

*W*ho is reaching out to secular people today? In Christendom, virtually all the people had a basic working knowledge of Christianity, had a positive attitude toward the faith, and assumed it to be true. The gospel's advocate had only to build on that and invite people to accept the faith. But today, after centuries of secularization, most people misunderstand Christianity, are negative (if not alienated) toward the Church, and do not assume the christian message to be God's supreme revelation. Our secular situation today is much like what the early apostolic church faced. As Donald Soper has observed:

Not one in every ten people has the remotest idea of what you and I within the church mean by 'religion.' . . . For most it is only another way of saying you mustn't run off the moral rails or you mustn't waste time and money on the pools. For many it is not even that, but a narrow-minded and not particularly attractive clique. Any other meaning simply doesn't get home to them. The Christian Church will have to walk before it can run toward a revival in this country; and by 'walking' I mean the patient explanation, over and over again, to the ordinary man and woman of what the Christian faith really is and what it offers—not what they take it to be. Only then can the appeal for personal surrender be honourably made.[1]

The Church thrived for a thousand years like a football team that always played with "home field advantage." Indeed, the Church defined the game, announced the rules, briefed the referees, and always had the crowd behind them, and the wind as well. All of that has changed. We occasionally play on a neutral field, and usually on the opponent's field—if we play at all. Unfortunately, most churches still sit back and wait for people to come play on the church's field. Donald Morgan observes that western society today is a free marketplace of ideas, and many people are open. The church is called to enter that market and compete for the minds of people, partly by "finding ways to take the high ground, so they have to deal with us and not relegate Christianity to obscurity and irrelevance." But who is doing that?

Unfortunately, in this new apostolic age, most Christians do not relate to secular people in a way that makes christian faith a live option. In the western Church, the Great Commission has become the Great Omission—for three reasons. First, many Church leaders are still oblivious to the changed map of the christian world mission today, and they persistently deny that western countries are now mission fields once again. Second, many church leaders do not yet share, as a deep and driving conviction, Samuel Shoemaker's declaration that "we have found a way of life which fully and entirely satisfies, and we do not care to keep it to ourselves. We believe that whatever has the possibility of helping somebody, has the warrant to be made public."[2] Third, many church leaders have lost, or never acquired, the vision of apostolic ministry to unbelievers in the West. Even those who believe in "apostolic succession" are likely to interpret this as ordination to mere chaplaincy services and teaching orthodox beliefs to the faithful. Very few ordained clergy and other christian leaders understand themselves, much less their congregations, as having inherited the work of the apostles to people who do not yet believe. In other words, many church leaders are afflicted with double myopia. They see neither their mission nor their mission field.[3]

THE APOSTOLIC JOB DESCRIPTION

By comparison, the earliest apostles and their colleague leaders and congregations saw their mission and mission fields with pristine clarity. The recorded early traditions about the apostles leave no doubt about their job description. That tradition does not picture the apostles primarily as church administrators or desk theologians. Primarily each was "sent out" (*apostello* in the Greek) into the world by the Holy Spirit, usually to a new field, area, or ethnic population, to extend the Church to people groups who had not yet received the opportunity. That was their vocation; and their congregations, once planted, continued the outreach.

As one sees that each apostle gave his life for the work of spreading the good news, the picture grows cumulatively clear. The tradition tells us that Peter took the gospel to Asia Minor, to the Jews who remained in Babylon, and in time to Rome—where he was crucified. Andrew established Christianity among the barbarian people of Scythia. Thomas preached and planted the Church among the stubborn Parthians, and he eventually founded Christianity in South India. Matthew proclaimed Christ in Anthropophagi, a land of cannibals, where they executed him—but the king's heart was moved as Matthew died; the king became a priest and led a movement of his own people into the faith. The tradition tells us that Philip was one of the great apostles to Asia, establishing Christianity in Athens, and in Hierapolis where he was executed. Simon the Zealot and Jude formed an apostolic team and communicated Christianity in Persia. James, the brother of John, was the apostle to Spain, where his body is yet buried. Bartholomew took Matthew's Gospel to India and preached there, and he eventually became the apostle to Armenia. The ancient tradition leaves us this astonishing description of Bartholomew:

He has black, curly hair, white skin, large eyes, straight nose, his hair covers his ears, his beard long and grizzled, middle height. He wears a white robe with a purple stripe and a white cloak with four purple gems at the corners. For 26 years he has worn these, and they never grow old. His shoes have lasted 26 years. He prays a hundred times a day and a hundred times a night. His voice is like a trumpet; angels wait upon him; he is always cheerful, and knows all languages![4]

While these marvelous post-biblical traditions about the apostles undoubtedly contain hyperbole, they leave no doubt about the apostolic job description. And they leave no doubt that their congregations were fully involved in gospel outreach; all baptized disciples were called to be fishers of men and women. Some very ordinary Christians even did pioneering apostolic work among new populations, such as those who spread the gospel in Antioch— where Gentiles first believed.

SIGNS OF APOSTOLIC RECOVERY

The recovery of the apostolic ministry of the clergy, and all the people of God, to peoples who do not yet believe is perhaps the most significant movement in the world Church in our lifetime. The Church in many lands is rediscovering that God entrusts evangelism, church planting, and cross-cultural mission to all disciples (not just religious professionals). When the vision of apostolic ministry is recovered, it is then expressed in some version of this pattern. An apostolic leader (or leadership group) reaches a remote tribe or an urban vocational group or some other distinct population—begins communicating the gospel, raises up some converts, forms them into a congregation, equips the congregation for its mission, grounds the people in the beliefs, life-style, and vision that inform and energize the mission, and eventually some of its members become apostles to other populations.

The *Lumen Gentium* document of the Second Vatican Council is a significant expression of the whole Church's recovery of apostolic vision and identity. The document declares that the doctrine of "Apostolic Succession" was instituted "in order that the mission assigned to [the apostles] might continue after their death . . . and . . . until the end of the world." The document defines the ongoing apostolic task as: "unceasingly to send heralds of the gospel until such time as the infant churches are fully established and can themselves carry on the work of evangelizing." The document explains that "the task of proclaiming the gospel everywhere on earth devolves on the body of pastors, to all of whom in common Christ gave His command," but the mission is carried out primarily through "the lay apostolate." *Lumen Gentium* affirms that "a lay apostolate has existed in the Church since the days of our Lord in Jerusalem," but "modern conditions demand that their apostolate be thoroughly broadened and intensified." Vatican II exempted no Christians from the apostolic imperative: "The obligation of spreading the faith is imposed on every disciple of Christ, according to his ability."

The recovery of apostolic identity and mission is often reflected in the ordination standards of christian movements who mean business. In eighteenth-century England, one of John Wesley's four tests for candidates for Methodist ministry was "fruits," that is, they had to have produced some converts. In much of Latin American Pentecostalism today, a ministry candidate must have raised up a flock of thirty believers before the denomination's leaders clear him or her for ordination.

THE "CHAPLAINCY TRAP"

In the West, however, most mainline, ordained ministers are more "chaplain" than "apostle." In a recent experience with one denominational judicatory's board of ordained ministry, one of several committees interviewing candidates for ordination began with this question: "Tell us about your appointment." The question is not as simplistic, or innocent, as it appears; what people choose to talk about is revealing.

An associate pastor reported personal spiritual growth and a good experience with the members. Another reported good relationships with the members and "gratifying" experiences in leading worship services. Another candidate, pastoring a recently merged church, reported that implementing the merger is "consuming" him. Another reported great meaning in word and sacrament, and "satisfaction" from involvement in ministries to various age groups. Another candidate found his appointment "comfortable," and "a blessing to our family." Still another reported fulfilment in teaching Scripture, and in officiating at weddings and funerals.

By now a pattern was emerging. Each candidate was focusing much more on his or her local church than upon the community the church is called to serve and reach; several candidates never referred to the community at all—though several referred to some denominational or ecumenical involvement beyond their local church. Furthermore, they were more enamored of the satisfactions they were receiving from ministry than of any outcomes, in the lives of people or in the life of the community, from their ministry.

When I probed interviewees with follow-up questions, an associate pastor shared a job description which emphasizes "visitation to members, shut ins, and hospitals," and working with the "young marrieds and singles" in several projects during Lent.

Someone asked: "What is the meaning of Lent?" After an

adequate textbook comment about the crucifixion and resurrection of Jesus, he added, "It was all for me."

I asked: "What about other people? Was it for them too?" "Yes, of course."

"For all other people, everywhere? Not just you and your church members?"

"Certainly."

"Is your job description consistent with that belief?" He said he assumed it was, because he inherited the job description from his predecessor!

Still another candidate, an "A" student from his Master of Divinity degree program, was pastoring a church in a transitional neighborhood; his members were moving out, people of a different subculture were moving in. I asked if they had received any new believers last year from the community; they had not. His answers to additional questions revealed that his church is not in regular conversation with any undiscipled people in the community, that he did not know how many are out there, that no such people are on the church's prospect list, in part because the church has no prospect list!

Finally, when we asked a candidate to tell us about her appointment, she began talking about the community and the needs and struggles that its people experience. She reported that a dozen people had joined the church as new Christians, that a handful of her members are now "ambassadors for Christ," and that much of the church has now developed "a conscience for world mission!" She had acquired this agenda after becoming a Christian in another country, and, as a course-of-study candidate, this one lone apostle was not a product of a seminary degree program.

So, from this sampling, one in nine candidates for ordination had primarily an outreach agenda for ministry. This sampling was roughly confirmed as I perused the essays on vocational ministry written by all 32 candidates. About 1 of every 8 or 9 or 10 emphasized service and/or witness to the community and/or to the world. The others were mainly focused inward upon their church.

A majority of ordained ministers in mainline denominations today are afflicted with amnesia. Christianity was launched as a movement of fishers of men and women; today, we are "keepers of the aquarium." While most of our churches would "like" to catch new fish, the only fish they really want to catch are fish already cleaned!

The founding geniuses of many denominations could have said, with John Wesley, "The world is our parish." Today, our parish is our world. Our clergy have little sense that they are ordained in "apostolic succession," that is, to succeed the original apostles in their mission to people and populations, and as leaders of apostolic congregations. The central roles of "professional ministry" today are widely defined, by pastors and by seminary curricula, as (1) leading worship, (2) preaching, (3) teaching, (4) counseling, and (5) administering.

While there is much to appreciate in this prevailing model for ministry, it seems curiously out of place—and it is. If you substitute "hearing confessions" for "counseling," the model is lifted almost straight out of Christendom, when all citizens were baptized and considered "Christians," when the Church and western culture were so yoked that the Church informed the culture's moral and ethical values, when the populations of Africa, Asia, Latin America, and Oceania had not yet been "discovered." In that medieval arrangement, where there was no perceived need for evangelism or world mission or social reform, the parish priest was, understandably, a mere chaplain to the settled christian community.

But that world of "Christendom," which the chaplain model once fit, no longer exists. After the Renaissance, the Reformation, the rise of nationalism, the rise of science, the Enlightenment, and urbanization, the entire western world is now substantially secularized. The secularization of the West is the most important contextual factor confronting the western Church. We are placed in a new apostolic age, warranting an apostolic model for the ministry of the people of God.

RECOVERING THE LAY APOSTOLATE

It is even more important to recover the apostolate of the laity than the apostolate of the clergy. Christianity first made an impact on the Roman Empire as a lay religious movement. Part of the apostolic truth that Martin Luther recovered was "the priesthood of all believers." The Anabaptist movement invested heavily in lay ministry and teaching of Scripture. John Wesley declared that

113

Methodism's mission was to spread the faith through the mission of lay preachers, class leaders, and many others who had "nothing to do but save souls," and who spent themselves in visiting from house to house, in marketplace conversations, in field preaching—in as many places as possible, in starting many new Methodist classes and societies, in inviting thousands of people to pursue and experience grace.

The recovery of lay apostolate and lay priesthood has occurred in nonwestern cultures as well. Twentieth-century Chinese Christianity has blazed its own trail. When Chairman Mao imposed the Cultural Revolution, there were only about one million Christians in all of China. The Cultural Revolution drove the christian movement underground, where it became indigenous, took on a "Chinese face," became lay led, and grew through an intentional proliferation of lay-led house churches. Today, Christians in China number from twenty to forty million. This great movement became possible because tens of thousands of laypeople, a majority women, discovered their calling to succeed the apostles in outreach to people who are not yet believers.

Our greatest imperative in the secular West is to recover the apostolic mission of the laity. Here, however, we encounter an entrenched problem: at least 90 percent of all congregations "delegate" evangelism and membership recruitment to the ordained minister; "That's your job, Pastor." There are at least three problems with this policy:

1. Despite a pastor's best motives and efforts, many of the people a pastor recruits do not, psychologically, join the church; they join the pastor! Therefore, when the pastor moves or retires, the people he or she recruited become inactive members and dropouts in disproportionate numbers; the magnet that drew them there, and the glue that once helped them stick, are now gone. We are learning that if the church really wants to attract, receive, and incorporate new members into the church, then the church must do the outreach.

2. The laity have a better opportunity than the clergy to reach undiscipled people. Donald McGavran's *The Bridges of God* helped us to see that the faith best spreads, within a social unit, across the kinship and friendship networks of vital believers. Church laity have many more bridges to undiscipled people than church professionals could ever duplicate.

3. We now know that evangelism may be the only enterprise where the "amateurs" outperform the "professionals!" According to Herb Miller's research with the National Evangelistic Association (Lubbock, Texas), when you compare the outreach, per 100 calls, of clergy and laity with similar gifts, the laity attract twice as many people into the faith, presumably because secular people do not perceive laity as being "paid" to invite them.

The results of the widespread delegation of outreach to the clergy is observed in the evangelistic impotence of most congregations. Consider, for instance, The United Methodist Church's recent record in receiving new Christians by profession of faith. In 1988, over 40 percent of the congregations (over 15,000 congregations) received not a single new Christian by profession of faith, not even one of their own children by confirmation. And, believe it or not, some congregations of 1,000 or more members received no new Christians that year. Such churches take care of their members, no doubt, and they welcome transfers; but they have no apostolic impact in the wider community.

Yet churches who believe in, and empower, the ministry of the laity are mighty forces. For instance, Alan Walker launched "Life Line" in 1963, deploying trained laypeople in telephone counseling. They advertised across Sydney that "help is as close as the telephone." They discovered that trouble, desperation, and suicidal feelings do not keep office hours, so the telephones soon were staffed 24 hours per day. By the early 1980s, the Life Line movement in Sydney was counseling about 60,000 callers per year, with 99 percent of the counseling by devoted laypeople who have made this ministry their avocation. Life Line spread to other Australian cities, then to New Zealand cities, and is now a worldwide movement, with over 200 centers in as many cities. By the mid-1980s, the movement was opening one new center per month.[5]

Life Line demonstrates that the most important ministries of a church to people can be entrusted to laity—with training, support, and recognition. The Life Line movement demonstrates, Walker says, that "the 'sleeping giant of the church' will awaken when the role of the laity is more specifically defined. It will come when the structure of the church is modified so as to use the followers of Christ in direct witness and service in the church and in the world.'"[6] Walker believes, with Emil Brunner, that "the minister church is finished," and deserves to be. If St. Peter is right that the whole Church is ''a royal priesthood,'' this ''ends forever the church as a two-class community, the ordained ministers and the people. It declares that the function of minister and people is the same.''[7]

Bruce Larson has long believed that the communication of Christianity to secular unchurched people happens primarily through the contacts, life, and witness of the laity in the world, and that the pastor's role is to call, equip, and deploy laypeople for their ministry in the world. When he arrived in 1980 as senior pastor of University Presbyterian Church in Seattle, he found a traditional conservative evangelical church which featured strong preaching and giving to missions. Even the congregation's 36 elders were only expected occasionally to read the scripture or say a prayer in a worship service, and the annual ''Laymen's Sunday'' implied a spectator role for the laity the other 51 Sundays. Larson was challenged to find ways to ''turn the church back to the people.'' He did it, and soon the church was receiving 400 new members per year, two-thirds as new believers. How did Larson help this happen? Generally, he ''discovered that people don't always do what you say, but they become what you call them. You tell them who they are, and if you are called to be their pastor, they tend to believe you.''

Programmatically, two broad initiatives shifted University Church's laity into the ministry of the laity. Larson discovered that evangelism was assigned to an evangelism committee, which meant that ''if ten people are doing it, then nobody else is doing it. But evangelism is everybody's job! So we disbanded the evangelism committee—which was a shock to our biblical, evangelical church! I said to the people, 'You are the ministers. Just tell the people where you live and work ''There is good news.'' We had no other program.' '' Then University Presbyterian Church's laity began practicing what the church had long preached.

Larson's other broad initiative involved great numbers of lay-people in actual cross-cultural mission experience. With an emphasis upon ''every member in ministry and every member in mission . . . we said 'If you are a member of this church, the day is going to come when it will be a requirement of membership for you to go on mission at least two weeks, every four or five years.' '' The people bought that challenge. Every department in the church, from junior highs, to senior highs, university students, singles, young married, and senior citizens began to send out teams. People who went last year, or plan to go next year, support the people going this year. From such involvement, "the whole church became mission focused; the whole church owned mission." In 1989, University Presbyterian Church sent out over 400 people overseas in mission—65 as career missionaries the church supports, 30 more giving a year to teach English as a second language, the others on two weeks to three months of mission experience with some Third World church. Larson reports: "Of course, they find that people who have nothing minister to them, and they come home transformed!"

Mission is both a means of transformation and a means of being transformed. So, some of the greatest folks in our church went on mission, and came home, and threw out their live-in lovers, and got their lives in order, and began to be new people—because of two weeks living in the Third World. . . . The whole idea is that we never know who we are and the power we have until we are involved in hands-on-mission and ministry to somebody. So mission is not just to help the world; it is also that you might find out who you are—and you might do some good along the way.

Moreover, those who return have gained the apostolic consciousness and conscience that permits them to see the mission field in Seattle and to affirm their role in reaching it!

With an apostolic identity, the whole People of God know that the main business of the Church is to serve and disciple people who do not yet believe and follow Christ. They refuse to buy the widespread assumption that ministry is basically chaplaincy services for people who are already Christians. The identity and role of Christians who reach out to secular people are rooted within the apostolic tradition. This is the first characteristic of Christians who communicate the faith to secular people.

The characteristics of Christians who reach secular people are of crucial importance, because if we can describe modern apostles accurately, specifically, and imaginatively, and if we rehearse the resulting model, we increase our possibility of becoming more like them. In addition to the apostolic identity of both laity and clergy, I have been able to identify, from relevant literature and field observations, thirteen other distinctive features of Christianity's most needed communicators.

PROFILING THE CHRISTIANS WHO REACH SECULAR PEOPLE

1. Christians on mission to secular society are familiar with some version of the story of the secularization of the West—at least the big picture. They understand that the christian movement no longer has the "home field advantage," and they can describe some of what this means and how the Church's strategy must change. Rick Warren suggests that the new question is "How can I get them to listen?"

In the past, this was no problem. The church was the biggest building in town, the pastor was the most important person in town, and the church program was the social calendar of the community. None of that is true anymore. The church building is dominated by skyscrapers. Pastors are low on the status pole. (On TV they are crooks or wimps.) And the social calendar of the community is not the church's program.

2. Christians who reach secular people are honest about themselves—in their relationships to themselves, to the Church, and to secular seekers. They know that, because they too live in the secularized western world, they too are painted by the brush of secularization and are affected by its assumptions and values. This honesty liberates them from a "holier-than-thou" stance, enables empathy with secular strugglers, and provides the foundation of realism for testifying to their faith in non-stylized ways that secular people can appreciate. When a secular woman asked Kenneth Chafin to tell what it is that Jesus Christ did for him "right now," he responded:

There are several things which Jesus Christ does for me right now. First, he helps me accept the fact that I am not perfect. I make mistakes. He forgives my sins day by day as I confess them to him. Second, he helps me to accept the gifts I have and to use them in a way that gives me a sense of fulfillment. Third, he helps me to love people that I would not have loved before. Fourth, he gives me good friends in the church who love me and care for me in all the circumstances of life. Fifth, he gives meaning to my life beyond my self. Finally, he helps me to accept the fact that I am mortal and will someday die. He gives me the hope of everlasting life through his resurrection.[8]

3. Modern apostles are people of faith, who deeply place their trust in God. Though their theology may be profound, they trust God with

a childlike trust, believing they are in God's hands, that God's purposes will prevail through them in God's good time. This relationship to God is reflected in a poem that Samuel Shoemaker wrote one evening after a leisurely walk with his first grandchild:

> He takes my hand, my little boy
> And feels as safe as safe can be;
> Talking as we walk along
> I with him, and he with me.
> I take my Father's hand in faith,
> Though where He leads, I may not see;
> My hand is given into His.
> I trust Him as my child trusts me.

And, because they live by the faith they commend to others, this helps establish their credibility.

4. But credibility involves more than genuine personal faith. The Church is rightly haunted by Nietzche's challenge: "I shall not believe in the Redeemer of these Christians until they show me they are redeemed."[9] Ralph Waldo Emerson observed that "the reason why anyone refuses his assent to your opinion, or his aid to your benevolent design, is in you. He refuses to accept you as a bringer of truth, because, though you think you have it, he feels that you have it not. You have not given him the authentic sign."[10] What gives the authentic sign?

Contagious Christians in a secular society are acutely aware of the credibility factor, but they know that genuine faith and consistency between public life and private life are only the beginning of credibility. Christians reaching for "the authentic sign" drive their roots deeper—by attending to their own spiritual formation, through means of grace such as Scripture, sacrament, and koinonia. Some Christians who lack the good sense to drive deeper for their own sakes know, nevertheless, to drive deeper for the sake of people to whom they commend the faith. They want all of the depth and grace God intends for them. They desire their own sanctification, for the sake of people to whom they communicate. Donald Soper discerns that "Christianity must mean everything to us before it can mean anything to others."[11]

Similarly, Alan Walker believes that "*we* must come to a greater experience of the Holy Spirit if we are to communicate to a lost world.'' He believes that Pentecostalism recovered a neglected part of the gospel that the whole Church needs, because ''the whole Church, especially 'mainline' Protestant Christianity, needs the Holy Spirit to liberate an impotent Church.'' The Holy Spirit is working in a situation before we enter it. This Spirit is awakening people and preparing their hearts to respond, and we are called to be sensitive to God's leading. The Holy Spirit empowers witnessing Christians for outreach, gives us the gift of transparent compassion, and gives us the words to say. This Spirit speaks God's living Word through our caring, listening, and speaking, and is the agent in conversion. Alan Walker reminds us that ''we do not take Christ to people; He is already there. We are only bearing witness to Him,'' and sometimes we are privileged to receive and gather the harvest He has prepared for Himself.[12]

5. Effective communicators to secular people have heroes or role models in apostolic ministry. Many of them caught their vision of an apostolic ministry from someone else, and all of them learned how to reach secular people, at least in part, from one or more role models. In some cases they knew their role models, and several were even mentored. Other communicators never knew their role model, but immersed themselves in their writings. Either way, they lit their apostolic candle at someone else's fire. I know of no modern apostles who came to it all by themselves, or reinvented apostolic ministry from scratch.

Donald Soper drew vision from models like John Wesley, Hugh Price Hughes, J. Ernest Rattenbury, and William Temple. Bryan Green stood in the proud Anglican evangelical tradition of Charles Simeon, read deeply in the works of Charles G. Finney, and was a confidante of Samuel Shoemaker. Robert Schuller drew widely for role models—including Shoemaker, E. Stanley Jones, Fulton J. Sheen, and Norman Vincent Peale. Alan Walker learned from observing his own father, a strong Australian evangelist; he also once worked with Soper at Kingsway Hall in London for a year. Bruce Larson experienced a mentoring relationship with Shoemaker, and drank from the wells of Paul Tournier and Elton Trueblood. Kenneth Chafin drew primarily from Trueblood, C. S. Lewis, and John Newport—the philosopher of religion under whom Chafin did his doctorate. Donald Morgan was deeply influenced by Samuel Shoemaker and Harry Emerson Fosdick, and studied homiletics at Union Theological Seminary with Ralph Sockman, George Buttrick, and Paul Scherer. Jim Harnish regards Robert Schuller, J. Wallace Hamilton, Garrison Keillor, and Fosdick as models from whom he has drawn selectively. Rick Warren learned a great deal from Fosdick and Schuller, even though he differs theologically from both. Their testimonies all confirm the maxim in leadership and management literature that "nobody makes it without a mentor," or at least a role model.

6. Effective apostles have clear objectives to achieve in their outreach to secular people. They manage their movements in terms of these objectives, and they often articulate the movement's objectives to the members. For instance, Bryan Green's goal for people is christian conversion—a change in which a person's face is now toward Christ, the person is now trusting the grace of God to justify his or her life, and a change in the person's consciousness—in which a person "who was not, now becomes a Christian in conscious and personal experience."[13] While the apostle may have many worthy hopes for people, he or she is clear about which hopes are not the primary objectives. So, Bryan Green reminds us that the primary objective for people is not theological indoctrination, religious experience, churchgoing habits, moral reform, or even social reform—but reconciliation to God.[14]

Samuel Shoemaker, in *The Experiment of Faith*, announces a similar objective: "To be . . . forgiven and accepted by Him is to be made whole, restored to par, set in accord; to be redeemed. To bring people this redemption through Christ is the primary concern of the Christian Religion. Righteousness is not its chief aim—that follows. Redemption is what we need, and what the Gospel sees we need."[15]

Shoemaker often spoke of the need for people to surrender to God's will in response to divine grace, and he saw the need for being sufficiently specific for people to understand what surrender involves. By drawing upon the faith's perennial perceptions of the human struggle, he saw the need for commitment to God's will around the three issues of "money, sex, and power. . . . Most people are not fixing to become monks; but if we are going to surrender to God, we must be specific about it; and these three—money, sex, and power—must be brought under obedience to Him.''[16] But the christian pilgrimage does not typically begin with total self-surrender to God; ''I know many persons who have begun by surrendering as much of themselves as they can to as much of Him as they understand.''[17] Indeed, Shoemaker often encouraged seekers to ''experiment with Christianity'':

You begin it . . . like you begin an experiment in physics or chemistry. You hear that if you mix two ingredients, a certain result will happen. You try it for yourself. If you are seeking a discovery that has not been made, you must take some hypothesis as being true, act as if it were true, and see what happens.
  The experiment of faith is just as simple, as accessible, as law-abiding as that. Begin reading your Bible. Begin going to church. Begin acting as if God were, by praying. If you feel doubt, tell Him so. Be honest. Call on Him when first you awaken in the morning. Say over the familiar things like the Lord's Prayer. Ask Him to use you this day, to guide you in working out the solutions to your problems, the knotty ones as well as the rest.[18]

Even so, employment of the conversion objective needs to be flexible, not stereotyped, because different personalities become Christians in different ways, as Bryan Green demonstrates from the lives of apostles and New Testament writers: John responded totally to Christ when he first met Him, Peter made the transition only after a number of false starts and crises, Paul had a sudden and dramatic conversion after having been a persecutor of the christian movement, and Timothy grew up as a Christian from childhood. The analogy of ''falling in love'' helps one understand variety in conversion. A couple may fall in love at first sight, another couple may make several attempts and experience several struggles before crossing the line for good, another couple may grow up close to each other and one day discover and make explicit their love. Likewise, ''conversion may be dramatic and apparently sudden,'' or it may ''come after much seeking and much struggling,'' or it may come as a person raised in a christian home and in the Church at last becomes aware of God in Christ as Savior and Master.[19] It really does not matter how it happens, what matters is only that it happens.

7. Effective christian apostles believe in the possibilities of people, by grace through faith. They do not write people off, no matter how

far people have fallen. Nor do they pretend that lost secular people are okay and are already fully aware of God's reconciling grace, because that false message reinforces the deepest fear of many people—the fear that who they become and how they live their life does not finally matter, even to God.[20] From the deep belief in people's possibilities, advocates from Wesley to Soper have addressed crowds and even mobs, believing in the possibilities of pagans, detractors, and even enemies. Shoemaker ministered to the most depraved urban dwellers that pious people could imagine, and launched Alcoholics Anonymous and similar ministries, because he knew what the grace of God can achieve in any life. Bruce Larson writes of Shoemaker that ''he recaptured the basic strategy of the New Testament, in that he was always impressed by the possibilities of the ordinary. He saw in ordinary men and circumstances the means and the weapons by which God could change the world.''[21] Schuller believes that our belief in people's possibilities functions in their lives like a self-fulfilling prophecy, as in *The Man of La Mancha*, when the harlot Aldonza becomes a lady of great dignity, Dulcinea—because Don Quixote saw her, and treated her, as Dulcinea.[22]

Always, the apostle has personal reasons for believing in the power of God's grace. Alan Walker, for instance, recalls that his own forebears immigrated to Australia as convicts. In 1810, a 26-year-old ancestor named John Walker was converted, was set free from ''the grip of alcohol,'' and began to preach Christianity as a life-changing power. Walker reports: ''I am the thirteenth . . . minister who has come from the conversion of John Walker. Our two sons are ministers of the gospel. Therefore, fifteen ministers of the gospel have come from the conversion of one illegitimate son of two convicts. Do you wonder why I believe in conversion?''[23]

A version of this radical belief in the possibilities of people is at the heart of the missionary enterprise. Whereas the evangelist is driven by belief in the possibilities of people, the missionary is driven by belief in the possibilities of a whole people. At least since Pope Gregory believed that the people called Angles could become ''angels,'' the vision of a people's possibilities has energized the missionary spirit.

8. Effective apostles study, analyze, and even research the population and culture they are called to reach. When I asked Alan

Walker, "What are the biggest mistakes Christians make in trying to reach unchurched people?" he identified the widespread "failure to analyze the society and the people to whom you are going." The reason this is important is self-evident. We are in no position to know the target population's culture, values, and life-style, or their felt needs, driving motives, and points of contact with Christianity, or their images, hangups, barriers, and doubts regarding Christianity, or the language they understand and the response patterns that are natural to them, or where and when they may assemble to consider the gospel—unless we find out! All of the apostles represented in this book pay the price to find out. They know, in Darrell Whiteman's words, that you have to "exegete the context as well as the text" if you intend to communicate the text's meaning to the people. So, Donald Soper, Bryan Green, Alan Walker, and Sam Shoemaker knew their respective cities as well as anyone. Donald Morgan has authoritative knowledge of New England history and culture. Rick Warren and Robert Schuller stay very informed and current on Southern California's cultures and trends.

The methods that modern apostles use to exegete the context vary from one apostle to another, and each relies on multiple channels. Robert Schuller and Rick Warren periodically survey targeted neighborhoods, door to door. Samuel Shoemaker learned a great deal about unchurched people through his two interviews with seekers per day, and Donald Soper through his two open-air meetings per week—exposed to people's questions, doubts, and challenges. Green, Soper, and Walker all developed and used city-wide networks of leaders who knew what was going on. Jim Harnish analyzes the movies people attend, and he is a perceptive observer and conversationalist at parties. Donald Morgan and Bruce Larson have degrees in psychology, and renew their knowledge through such publications as *Psychology Today*. Robert Schuller listens to the news, reads secular magazines and newspapers, and joins secular clubs. Rick Warren reads books on contemporary American history and culture, and subscribes to *American Demographics*. They are (or were) all active pastors, intentionally learning from the people and community in the midst of ministry. Alan Walker claims that "there is a level of pastoral life, below which you cannot fall, if you are going to be an effective pastor."

9. Effective apostolic communicators identify with the people they are called to reach. Like Agnes Liu of Hong Kong, they learn as much as they can about their lives, struggles, values, attitudes, beliefs, worldview, heroes and heroines. Expressing the incarnational model, they come to understand what life looks and feels like within the experience of the target population. They help articulate the people's grievances and champion their causes in the wider community—as in Soper's public advocacy on behalf of unemployed dock workers, Shoemaker's defense of addicted people, and Schuller's apologia for people with low self-esteem; the people feel the spokesman is on "our side." These advocates work with the people—as co-laborers—in jobs, causes, and community activities. The modern apostle likes secular unchurched people, enjoys them, finds them interesting, believes in their possibilities—and that communicates. These apostles even identify with the people in their friendships, play, and recreation.

Many evangelicals who think of sinners in the world as little more than "souls with ears" would never guess how much this relational identification means to people. One pastor plays basketball two afternoons per week with neighborhood teenage boys. One day as two members of the church were walking by the church's outdoor basketball court, they saw the pastor miss a jump shot. One woman paused, her mood changed, and she asked her friend, "Where was that pastor when my boy was growing up?"

10. Because people are much more than souls with ears, effective apostolic congregations are not involved in witness alone. They are involved, perhaps even more, in ministries to a range of human needs. In the late 1960s, when Donald Soper was still superintendent of the West London Methodist Mission, the mission was expressed through a remarkable range of thirteen service institutions, including a thrift shop and homes for alcoholics, unmarried expectant mothers, young people, and retirees.

Alan Walker, as a young man, worked and learned at the West London Methodist Mission, returned to his native Australia, and led Sydney's Central Methodist Mission into an era of extensive social ministries, involving a *staff* of over 500! Walker learned that ministries and institutions like christian children's homes, retirement homes, nursing homes, hospitals, halfway houses, etc. should, whenever possible, be linked to a local church rather than to a denomination or judicatory. These ministries enabled the Central Methodist Mission to bring many people into faith, because "the deed of the gospel gains credibility for the Word." Walker believes that, in our secular world, "There is no future for a [merely] talking Christianity."

In addition to the Crystal Cathedral's multiple 12-Step support groups for nine addictive populations, the church features support groups for survivors of suicide, professionals in transition, cancer conquerors, growing through grief, friends against depression, single mothers, single fathers, physically challenged people, men with anger control problems, people caring for an elderly parent, stroke recoverers, parents of gay children, parents of adopted children, teens of divorcing parents, and victims of incest.

Such churches are, of course, communicating while they are ministering, and the ministries establish the church's credibility, influence people's attitudes, and serve as signs of God's goodness and compassion. The compassionate congregation creates a climate conducive to the discovery of faith.

11. Most effective communicators of Christianity to secular people develop a point of view, a set of *driving, core convictions*, that they communicate over the decades. These communicators do not pretend to represent equally all points of truth in the Scripture and in christian tradition. They are gripped by a "magnificent obsession," deeply convinced of certain truths for people to believe and realities for them to experience. For instance, much of Robert Schuller's contribution is due to the fact that he is obsessed to see defeated people discover the God-given possibilities before them, and to believe in themselves because God does. In contrast, Donald Soper's obsession has been to recover the social relevance of the christian faith in our post-christendom age. Soper's message has been consistently rooted in the doctrine of the Kingdom of God, with its expression unusually specific: for Soper, the programmatic expression of the Kingdom of God would be a form of democratic socialism and pacifism. His consistent vision is memorably captured in this 1937 discourse:

Before the Church challenges anybody else to accept its faith in God it
must . . . declare what is the Christian form of social life and must refuse to
support any other. . . .

I want men to know that by giving their allegiance to Christianity they will
be embarking upon a great campaign to banish war and poverty and injustice,
to overthrow the false and corrosive doctrines of State, Empire, and race
purity, and to set up a communal life where love and service have taken the
place of selfishness and armed might.

But just as important, I want the Church which sends out this manifesto to
be the "advance copy" of that new world it preaches.[24]

I asked every christian communicator that I interviewed to
"summarize your own christian message, or emphasis, for secular
unchurched people." Every advocate had a ready and articulate
response. For instance, Ken Chafin believes that

essentially, that in back of all existence—this whole world and everything in
it, is a powerful, personal, purposeful Being—who is Creator of the
universe. He is in back of creation. This Person has revealed himself to us in
Jesus Christ. He revealed that God purposes for each of us Life in all of its
fulness, and that you will never know that Life outside of a relationship with
God. . . . You keep working on it all you want to, and accumulate all you
want to—you are not going to know the Life that you were made for, apart
from Jesus Christ.

Rick Warren commented at length on three basic lines of thought
that secular people need to be in touch with: (1) that God is a personal
God, and cares about you and your life; he wants a relationship with
you, in which He knows you and you know Him; (2) that God is in
control, and the things that are out of your control are not out of His
control; (3) that you cannot control the things that happen to you, but
with the Holy Spirit's guidance and power, you can control your
response.

Jim Harnish stressed five affirmations for secular seekers: (1) God
is good. (2) God understands you. (3) God has already won the
victory in Christ. (4) God is involved in this world. (5) the Church has
a role in this, as the Body of Christ and the community of faith with a
mission in the world.

Bill Hybels frames much of his essential message within two
affirmations: (1) "You matter to God, no matter how far you have

fallen, no matter how many of His laws you have broken.'' (2) "The Christian life is not just a way to prepare to die. It is the better way to live, the straightest, truest path toward human satisfaction and fulfillment, even though it is very demanding and challenging along the way.''

Bruce Larson explains his gospel emphasis by contrasting it to mere orthodoxy:

> When Jesus started the Church, he gathered twelve people and said "Follow me"—which means that truth is a person, not a concept. God in Christ asks "Will you change who runs your life?" So conversion is not just accepting a high Christology; conversion is giving up your self-centeredness, and letting Jesus become the living center of your life, and becoming a part of what Jesus is doing in the world.
>
> In this sense, the Church is full of unconverted people who have a high Christology. So, many "Christian" people, even "evangelical" people, live like the outsider lives.

Larson shows how this perspective is expressed in interpersonal witness: "When a person is seeking, don't try to sell him your brand of theology or ethics or the doctrine of your church. Simply say in some form, 'Well, if you want to meet Christ, he's here and he loves you. He died for you, he wants to live in you. If you're tired of running your own life and you want him to take over, tell him and I will be your witness.''[25]

The lengthy careers of Soper, Schuller, Green, Walker, Larson, and others illustrate a central feature of effective advocates: They do not change their minds every few years. This does not mean that they parrot the messages of earlier years. They develop, over time, a rhetorical arsenal for communicating their consistent driving convictions; they develop the capacity to express the same idea in a hundred ways. The ideas are not static; they evolve within a reflective maturing mind. Commitment to a consistent, if evolving, message does not even preclude appreciation for other points of view. But effective advocates are not easily deflected from their course, because, as G. K. Chesterton suggested, the Church that changes its mind on the Truth every few years cannot be a great movement, much as social idealists, who flit from one cause to another, never change anything.[26]

Great advocates develop a consistent message because many people have conceptual needs. Christianity's primary realities are (1) volitional—a commitment to Christ and God's will, (2) experiential—from second birth through sanctification, and (3) relational—a new relationship to God, others, the world, and the self. Many people need *first* to see "God's blueprint" or "the landscape of reality before they can be gripped by God."[27] Many people need to make sense of their lives, to glimpse the purpose of life and history, or to gain a comprehensive and satisfying worldview before they can commit to Christianity (or any religion, philosophy, or cause); or at least they need to know that such a conceptual structure is behind the faith. Until recently, Communism was the great world demonstration that a clear coherent vision of purpose within history could engage and mobilize many people; Communism's sudden demise demonstrates that no movement can be forever sustained if the consistent experience of its people is contrary to the vision. So the role of christian philosophy has an enduring role in christian witness. All effective apostles love God with their minds and speak a faith that makes sense.

12. Though their christian philosophy and core convictions are constant, effective communicators of the faith do not simply announce their convictions and let people "take it or leave it." They are apostles and also "apologists." They engage in reasonable conversation with seeking people. They know that post-enlightenment people have doubts, questions, and challenges that must be honestly addressed before an experiment of faith is possible. They also know that secular western culture, like any culture, has an imprinted "mind" of its own; its individuals play their culture's "tapes" in challenging the christian advocate, so the communicator engages the mind of the culture. For example, when a heckler needles Donald Soper about "too many hypocrites in the Church," Soper knows that the individual is not presenting a conclusion from original field-research but a tape from the cultural script. Effective communicators take the culture's mind seriously; they learn its values, attitudes, beliefs, and assumptions; they learn its images, hangups, and stereotypes of Christianity. Then the advocate is prepared to respond to the culture's challenges to Christianity by developing communicable answers to these challenges, and by

engaging in reasonable conversation with the folk mind of their culture.

Perhaps half of an open-air meeting with Donald Soper is devoted to responses to these "taped," or stereotypical, challenges. His answers function in an apologetic role, helping the audience to see that Christianity makes sense. The following exchanges are typical:

Questioner: We do not feel any necessity for postulating a God. Cannot everything be explained ultimately in materialist terms?
Soper: That is your belief. But is not the mind that has found these things out more wonderful than the things themselves? . . . You say that everything comes out of matter. I think that everything we know comes through matter. . . . You might argue that playing the violin is merely applying the outside of a horse to the inside of a cat, but music is not just so much catgut and horsehair. They are but the media through which we enjoy it. This material universe is the instrument upon which we play and through which comes the music of achievement and happiness.

Questioner: What evidence is there, outside the Bible, that Jesus ever lived at all?
Soper: If all the reputable evidence is collected and put under one cover—and that is exactly what the Church did—surely it's not surprising that you won't find it elsewhere.

Questioner: You say you are a Christian and out for peace. How do you explain the fact that after 2,000 years of Christianity we had the worst war in history?
Soper: But have we had 2,000 years of Christianity? Surely Chesterton is right when he says: "Christianity has not been tried and found wanting—it's been found difficult and left untried."

Questioner: We judge Christianity as we find it.
Soper: Undoubtedly; but have you found it? Surely the Church is more than an institution; it is a living fellowship, and you can never judge a fellowship from the outside.[28]

Such exchanges are important within ministry to a secular population, because most secular people assume that a favorite, pre-recorded challenge settles the matter against Christianity and the Church—until a plausible rejoinder reopens the matter. That is why the advocate's studied answers are important; such answers help to keep the conversation alive, and to inform people, change attitudes, establish Christianity's good sense, and nourish the adoption process.

Samuel Shoemaker focused especially on those culturally scripted questions and doubts that keep people from "the experiment of faith." In one book he shared some answers he used in evangelistic interviews:[29]

To people who protest that they are not the "religious type," Shoemaker acknowledges that "Sometimes we think faith is given to some people and not to others, like an ear for music, or a striking personality. [But] Faith is much more like falling in love, which can come to anybody. Faith does not so much depend on my capacity to give it as on the other person's capacity to arouse it. . . . It is my belief that nobody can stay around our Lord Jesus Christ very long without coming to believe in Him. The faith is mine, but it is provoked by Him. Faith is my response to Him" (p. 68).

To people who aren't sure that they understand enough theology, or even understand themselves enough, to make a commitment, Shoemaker prescribes "Don't begin with what you *don't* believe; begin with what you *do* believe. . . . We begin the actual Christian experience when we surrender as much of ourselves as we can to as much of Christ as we understand (pp. 69-72).

When someone protests "whether it is fair to come to God when you're in a jam?" Shoemaker prescribes a "ready answer. . . . Suppose you had a son who went out to the ends of the earth somewhere, and lost himself, and one day you had a cable from him asking for help—what would you do? . . . Chances are you would send him something to get home with, and give him another chance. Don't you think God is at least as good as you are (pp. 25-26)?

To the suggestion that "education will save the world," and what people really need is education, Shoemaker observes with George Buttrick that "the real aim of education 'cannot be different from the total purpose of life,'and that the 'major question that education must face . . . is God.'. . . Men do not only need facts: they need the interpretation of facts, which involves faith, for no value emerges from facts alone, nor do facts arrange themselves in any meaningful pattern. Education of the kind we have been seeing will *not* save the world" (pp. 19-20).

To the suggestion that science will save the world, Shoemaker asks, "Is science a full account of things? What about man's imagination and purpose? What about ideals and values? What about a First Cause behind all this? It seems increasingly clear that science only describes processes, but says nothing of origins or destinies, or of the value of one fact as against another. No man ever fell in love, or wrote a good poem, or threw himself

131

into a lake to save a child, or exiled himself in the heart of Africa like Schweitzer to atone for the white man's sins against the black, without bringing into play forces which science can neither create nor altogether explain'' (p. 24).

To the suggestion that ''there are too many hypocrites in the Church!'' Shoemaker explains ''that on its human side the Church is not a museum but a school or even a hospital, not a place where people are on exhibition or parade, but a place where they are learning how to live. They haven't arrived—they are traveling, we hope in the right direction. But the Church on its divine side is a source of spiritual power, and we go back to it when we need a refill'' (pp. 88-89).

While an apologetic role is necessary in reaching secular people, it has its limits; so when the communicator approaches the limits of good reason in influencing a person, the communicator makes sure to leave the ball in the other person's court. Donald Soper admits to a seeker: ''I can't argue you to a belief in Jesus Christ; what I have tried to do is to offer you reasonable grounds for taking Him seriously. The next step is with you. I can't prove that He is the Master—He alone can do that, and He will. If you will really get to know this Jesus of history, you will find that He is the explanation of all that He taught and the vindication of every claim He made.''[30]

13. Effective apostolic communicators are characterized by a remarkable persistence in pursuing their apostolic vision, in believing in people's possibilities, in identifying and ministering, in communicating, reasoning, and conversing. They share this trait in common with all other effective leaders. They prevail and achieve their goals by determination and endurance, with what Admiral Rickover called ''courageous patience.''

This quality of persistent vision drove Robert Schuller to plant his roots for his whole life in a highly unchurched county in California; persistent vision drove Samuel Shoemaker into offices, homes, joints, and alleys year after year; persistent vision has driven Donald Soper to his soap box for six decades. Neither the world nor ordinary Christians can quite understand the awesome persistence with which such apostles maintain their vision and adhere to their mission. It is possible for any of us to seek with all our hearts that gift of persistence. Such persistence is reflected in William Booth's spiritual battlecry:

While women weep, as they do now, I'll fight.
While little children go hungry, as they do now, I'll fight.
While men go to prison, in and out, in and out, as they do now, I'll fight.
While there is a poor lost girl upon the streets,
While there remains one dark soul without the light of God,
    I'll fight. I'll fight to the very end.

What Kind of Church Reaches Secular People?

*T*he "map" of the christian world mission has changed. This fact has been established for several decades, but previous christian generations denied it; our generation is the first to experience the paradigm shift that makes it possible to take this fact seriously. Once, the countries and peoples of Europe and North America were "Christian" and the countries and peoples of the Third World were "mission fields." That picture has changed dramatically. Due to the discipling of many Third World nations and the secularization of the West, a higher percentage of Uganda's citizens are active professing Christians than citizens of the United States, a higher percentage in South Korea than in Canada, a higher percentage in Fiji than in any country in Europe. The United States has become the largest mission field in the western hemisphere, and most of the countries of Europe are almost secular wastelands.

Because the traditional mission sending nations of the western world are now "mission fields" once again, our greatest priority is to raise up a very great number of intentional missionary congregations. Such congregations will no longer be content to merely nurture and counsel the diminishing ranks of the faithful; their primary mission will be to reach people who do not yet believe, to make the christian faith, life, and mission a live option for undiscipled people.

More missionary congregations for the West will be required than anyone is now imagining, much less planning. For example, if we estimate, for the United States alone, at least 120 million secular unchurched people (aged fourteen or older) who will not be reached by traditional congregations, what would it take to bring to faith even half of these people within the next decade? If we imagine a host of apostolic congregations averaging five new believers per month, or sixty new believers per year, it would take one hundred thousand such churches to disciple sixty million people in a decade. Where would such churches come from? Perhaps fifty thousand of the present 360 thousand churches in the United States would catch the vision and move "from tradition to mission." The other fifty thousand would be new churches, intentionally planted to reach secular populations.

Providentially, we do not begin this quest from scratch. Some pioneering churches, like Willow Creek Community Church in the Chicago area, where Bill Hybels is senior pastor; Saddleback Valley Community Church in Southern California, where Rick Warren is senior pastor; and other churches featured in this book are demonstrating some ways forward. But why do these churches, and a comparative handful of the other 360,000 congregations, gather grain in harvest fields where most churches come out empty handed? Can we "profile" the kind of church that reaches secular people?

The answer is yes, and the most important single insight is that these churches have not "reinvented church." They have largely drawn from, and adapted, ideas and models that have been available in relevant literature for a quarter of a century—ideas that most churches have ignored while perpetuating church-as-usual in a changing culture.

Bruce Larson has pioneered many of the ideas that effective congregations seem to have drawn from. Larson and Ralph Osborne, in 1970, published *The Emerging Church*.[1] The churches they called for did not emerge in great numbers in the 1970s, but more emerged in the 1980s. The 1960s had already branded traditional forms of church life as "archaic" and "irrelevant." Larson and Osborne were already seeing that the mere "renewal" of the conventional church would not do. "Not renewal but a new thing. . . . That 'new thing' must find its own authentic form, life-style, and purpose."[2]

Naturally, a church's first challenge is to transcend the usual stream of parish problems which, like squeaking wheels, always get priority attention in the life of the typical church:

In a typical parish, the choir is invariably short of tenors, or some irritation has resulted from poor congregational attendance at the latest cantata. The women's association nominating committee never seems to find the right persons for all the available jobs. The church school is perennially short of good teachers, and most of the classroom furnishings would not be acceptable in a second-rate public school system. Funds are always in short supply. And dear Mrs. So-and-So is forever able to communicate effectively that "the pastor has not called on me lately."

There is no shortage of problems. An entire career can be maintained solely at the problem level, with the pastor no more than an ordained mechanic racing from problem to problem with his little bag of ecclesiastical tools. In those brief periods when all of the machinery seems to be meshing smoothly, he frantically catches his breath and waits for an S.O.S. call from the next disaster area. If your goal for ministry is being able to handle problems efficiently, you are scarcely describing the concept of ministry portrayed in the Book of Acts![3]

Churches discover the perspective to transcend the day-to-day syndrome by moving with a threefold agenda.

RELATIONAL THEOLOGY

First, Bruce Larson saw that relational goals for people (supported by a Relational Theology) liberate churches from much parish stagnation, because "it is our goals, conscious or unconscious, which largely determine what direction our lives take, and whether we find freedom and fulfillment."[4] In *The Emerging Church*,[5] Larson and Osborne introduce four themes that Larson advances in later writings, especially *No Longer Strangers*,[6] and *The Relational Revolution*.[7] Larson focuses on our relationship to God, our relationship to ourselves, our relationship to the "significant others" in our lives, and our relationship to the world, because "the quality of these relationships determines whether one truly *lives* or merely muddles through life."[8] Most churches reaching unchurched people have implemented such a relational focus.

The first relational goal involves a person's relationship to God. Jesus Christ responds to people's sin and estrangement by offering a new relationship with God—characterized by God's love, grace, and forgiveness, and our trust, obedience, and enjoyment of God's presence. Following Sam Shoemaker, Larson sees the new saving relationship to God beginning when we respond to God's unconditional love by committing to God all that we can. God then begins to work in us to make us transformed, transparent, relatable persons. We discover that Christianity is not basically beliefs about God or keeping God's rules, but a new relationship with God. "When

Jesus Christ says 'I love you unconditionally. Will you give me your life?' we cannot respond to this with 'true' or 'false' any more than we can respond to the statement, 'I love you. Will you marry me?' by saying 'true' or 'false.' We can only say 'yes' or 'no.' ''[9]

The second relational goal involves a new relationship with our inner selves—characterized by honesty, acceptance, and appreciation. People have the need to affirm themselves because most people are hounded by feelings of low self-worth. God's revelation that we are of immense value to God frees us to affirm ourselves. ''When this news finally gets through to me in Jesus Christ, I am caught with the simple observation that if God loves me this much, there must be something in me that is lovable.''[10] This discovery frees us to be less self-preoccupied, to see ourselves realistically, to affirm ourselves, to be our real selves, to be free from our defense mechanisms, and to be less dependent upon approval from others; and our self-affirmation frees us to relate differently with other people and the world. ''Jesus understood our need for self-love. He commanded us to love our neighbor *as* ourselves. One cannot love his neighbor until he loves himself, so it is crucial that we accept the love of God for us in our badness as well as in our goodness.''[11] Admittedly, self-love does not come easy; it takes the power of God within us.

The third relational goal involves a new relationship with the ''significant others'' in our lives—characterized by openness, vulnerability, and affirmation. Larson reminds us that ''there are individuals in the world besides ourselves, and some of these will not be ignored. We are married to them, we have given birth to them, we work with them, we socialize with them. We may relate badly to the 'significant others' in our lives, but we cannot make them go away.''[12] Humanity's usual relational style involves manipulative, controlling, ''straightenerouter'' tactics—from marriage and parenting, to business and government. But the consequences of the manipulative life-style are loneliness and alienation. God's revelation in Christ offers the distinctive christian life-style for relating to people we live and work with: We are called (1) to affirm others—seeing and bringing out the best within them, and (2) to be vulnerable to others—giving up defensive, self-protective, critical ways for openness about our feelings, failures, and need for help. Larson observes:

The Church . . . ought to be the place in which man begins to find God's answer for him in terms of a deep, loving, meaningful, relationship with the significant others in his life. But in the Church, sadly enough, we find people either denying their loneliness because it seems to them to be somehow 'unchristian' or pretending to be better than they are and shutting the door to meaningful relationships based on honesty and transparency.

No one is more lonely than two Christians living together or working side by side and pretending to be better than they are. Some of the most astonishing miracles I have seen have occurred when Christians have stopped playing games and dared to appropriate the power that God has made available in Christ. Because of this power, they have dared to love each other enough to reveal those things about themselves that could be threatening or damaging.[13]

The fourth relational goal involves a new relationship with the world—characterized by identification, involvement, and service.[14] Too often, believers merely enjoy Christ's benefits and each other, while either ignoring a world of hunger, poverty, superstition, oppression, possession, and lost people or "helping" the world (like writing a check) without getting involved. So the Christ who died for the world calls God's people to join in ministry amidst its struggles. Larson believes that every Christian needs two conversions: one out of the world (from its false values, immorality, and idolatry), and a second back into the world (in mission). Disciples in mission become involved with people and communities as Jesus did. "The earth is the Lord's and the fulness thereof," so the Lord calls disciples to join God in that world to love, reclaim, redeem, and change the world, that other people might be reconciled to God and that God's will might be done on earth. We are also called to redemptive involvement with the world for our sakes, because Jesus meets and completes us through the neighbor in need.[15]

The salient objective, then, of the relational church is for all people to have the opportunity to experience the new relationships with God, self, significant others, and the world that the gospel and God's power make possible. Consequently, Bruce Larson believes that the theological support for such a mission must come from a "Relational Theology." Reacting to the impotence of the more sterile forms of orthodoxy, Larson suggests that

the Bible deals primarily with relationships and only indirectly with doctrine. . . . Reading the Bible convinces me that the real test of "orthodoxy" has to do with the quality of relationships far more than with doctrinal stands. Life's real problems are obviously relational; they are only indirectly doctrinal. . . . Certainly [doctrine] may explain to a degree what sin is, and what grace is, but doctrine *per se* is not the very stuff of life. It merely describes life without enabling it. . . . We are not trying to make people believe "the right things" so much as enabling them to experience a relationship with God and with one another.[16]

Larson cites Alcoholics Anonymous as a movement practicing a relational theology that informs the way members love and care for one another in ways that release power and new life. "AA, though doctrinally questionable by Christian standards, is relationally sound. The Church ought to be both! It is tragic that we in the Church are forced to choose between doctrinal soundness and relational soundness."[17]

LAY MINISTRY

Second, Larson and Osborne foresaw that an empowered relevant Church would feature the ministry of the laity in the world. "There will be no second-class Christians in the emerging Church. Neither will there be 'professional Christians' through whom the rest of us live out our faith vicariously."[18] All laity will be challenged, trained, and deployed to serve and witness using their spiritual gifts. Larson wrote, in 1967, that "God is raising up a lay ministry which is causing an upheaval in the Church comparable to the Copernican revolution."[19] That revolution, today, is advanced in the churches reaching secular people.

Bruce Larson suggests that the transcending congregation will find three New Testament words—*kerygma*, *koinonia*, and *diakonia*—to be the biblical keys for understanding the ministry of all Christians.[20] Kerygma refers primarily to the essential message of apostolic Christianity about God's saving reconciling deeds in the ministry, death, and resurrection of Jesus Christ, and secondarily to the whole Word of God in Scripture. Koinonia refers to the rich fellowship with other Christians, especially a fellowship in depth with a few other Christians. Diakonia refers to the service of the people of God in the world, and includes justice and deeds of mercy, as well as witness. Larson quotes Sam Shoemaker's version of this formula: "Get changed, get together, and get going.'' Larson believes that all three of these realities—conversion, meaningful fellowship, and finding a ministry—are essential for a complete christian life.[21]

We can see why each of these, kerygma, koinonia, and diakonia, is essential when we observe people trying to live as Christians without it. Ken Chafin once discussed the role of fellowship with some Baptist leaders in Mississippi. He asked whom they would want to know if they ever got in trouble—if their son was in jail or their daughter was pregnant. A sadness came over the room. One person, speaking for the group, said, ''I don't know who I'd like to know first, but I know who I'd like to know last. I'd like for the people of the church to be the last to find it out.''[22]

We can appreciate why all three are necessary when we review what we understand about the complexity of personality and human nature. Take, for example, Abraham Maslow's hierarchical under-standing of human motivation:[23]

> Worldview Needs
> Aesthetic Needs
> Self-realization Needs
> Esteem Needs
> Love and Belonging Needs
> Safety and Security Needs
> Physiological Needs

Maslow theorized that all of those needs are present in human personality, but not all are currently active and driving a person's behavior. The ''lowest'' level of essentially *unmet* needs drives a personality until those needs are essentially met; so, for instance, a sleep deprived or malnourished man is currently driven by these physiological needs, and he is not primarily concerned about a job promotion or acquiring tickets to the symphony. A ''higher'' motivational force energizes a person when the lower needs are essentially met; so, a woman whose physiological, security, affiliation, and esteem needs are essentially met is probably trying to get in touch with her potential and asking questions about meaning and purpose for her life.

Maslow's hierarchy helps us perceive why all three of the resources of *kerygma*, *koinonia*, and *diakonia* are needed in a church's ministry. No one of these resources engages all of the human needs within the full spectrum of human personality. Koinonia, for instance, is capable of addressing people's affiliation and esteem needs, but has less relevance for safety and self-realization needs, and little obvious relevance for physiological or worldview needs. Kerygma addresses some of these needs more obviously than others, and diakonia engages others. So the church that industriously involves its people and seekers in all three of these resources is more likely to engage the whole person than is a church that inordinately relies on preaching or small groups or lay ministries. The inclusion of aesthetic needs within our understanding of human motivation helps us appreciate why some christian leaders add *leitourgia* (worship) as a fourth indispensable resource of the gospel.

Maslow's motivational hierarchy enables us to gain some other strategic insights. For instance, Robert Schuller's Crystal Cathedral is famous for effectively engaging people whose self-esteem needs are driving them; this is the church's magnificent obsession, and it has undoubtedly identified a massive, and neglected, market. But it helps explain why people who are somewhere else on the hierarchy of motives may not be attracted to Schuller's preaching or church. And it may help explain why the Crystal Cathedral has experienced its fair share of "graduates"—that is, people who once joined and became Christians but who later transferred their membership to another church. *If* the Crystal Cathedral were inattentive to the self-realization and worldview needs of its people whose former esteem needs have been met, it would lose people as they move up the hierarchy and experience a different motivational agenda than the one that first brought them to the Crystal Cathedral's esteem-related ministries.

All of this underscores what Bruce Larson suggested a quarter century ago in *Setting Men Free*: that Christians-in-the-making become, in John Wesley's words, "people of One Book"; that they live "in deep fellowship with a few other Christians," that they serve Christ by serving people in the world, and especially that they turn the management of their lives over to Jesus Christ.[24] Larson used the triad for diagnosing struggling churches. He saw that some of the fundamentalist churches were "all kerygma—but not much life." Some unity churches "enjoy all their hugging—but no kerygma." And some of the liberal churches "are out there picketing and organizing food banks"—while burning out and declining in numbers. So, "you put the three together for significant life change."

Larson became more obsessed with these themes when he assumed leadership of Seattle's University Presbyterian Church in 1980. He explained to his people that "the invitation is to Christ *and* to small groups *and* to mission":

> My challenge to them was not coercive, or hard sell, or confrontive. I just said, "Are you happy with what you are doing? If you are not, then listen. It is as important for you to belong to a small group as to believe that Jesus died on the cross for you. He cannot give you the abundant life promised in John 10:10 unless you believe that you are forgiven, and you walk away from your shady past—that we all have, and unless you get into a small group where God, through some people, can love you, encourage you, set you free, and tell you who you are. And, you have got to be involved in mission—for your sake." People bought that! Nobody argued with me about that!

CHURCH STRATEGY

Third, Larson and Osborne's *Emerging Church* also challenged churches who wanted a viable future to take *strategy* seriously.[25] From time to time, every church needs to change its strategy— because the surrounding culture has changed; but most churches merely perpetuate inherited strategies that once were valid but have now become programs demanding support. According to Larson and Osborne, strategy development begins with vision, because "the vision . . . gives shape and direction, dignity and force, to all that is happening within a faithful congregation."[26] The vision then suggests the specific approaches to ministry that will enable the church to achieve the objectives of its mission. Many church leaders would be sobered to read Larson and Osborne's reflections on specific ministries, because the stereotypical approaches to evangelism, preaching, christian education, and worship they exposed as inadequate for the 1970s are blindly perpetuated in nine of ten churches today!

Though every church has its unique personality, strengths, and opportunity, and therefore its unique strategy, Larson and Osborne identify one strategic component that characterizes the emerging church everywhere—"the emergence of the lay apostolate as God's primary means of accomplishing His will in the world."[27] They identify four strategic areas of church life for developing a lay apostolate: (1) worship, (2) small groups, (3) retreat program, and (4) serious training. Their agenda for a regular weekly small group meeting, which is brilliantly consistent with John Wesley's eighteenth-century class meetings, could release and empower many laypeople in every church in the western world:

1. Have a time "when people can open their hearts to one another and talk about their past failures and present hopes."
2. Have a time for "dialogue" and encounter wherein members can discern gifts among one another which might never be discerned otherwise. It is amazing how limited we are in seeing ourselves without the help of others.
3. Have each member identify "the particular thing to which God is calling them for the week ahead."
4. Hold each other accountable.[28]

The future, more than ever, is "wide open for churches that see themselves as centers for recruiting, training, and equipping a breed of spiritual pioneers competent to move out into all areas of life as lay apostles who can evangelize, reconcile, and prophesy."[29]

Although many of the major themes and insights that inform effective churches reaching secular people today have been advocated for more than twenty years, the literature of 1970 did not anticipate every component of contagious congregations for the 1990s and beyond. Churches like Saddleback Valley Community Church, in Orange County California, and Willow Creek Community Church, in metropolitan Chicago, reflect some recent discoveries and insights. Their contribution to other churches can be addressed by two questions: (1) What do the bellwether churches that reach secular people *know* or take seriously that most other churches do not know or take seriously? (2) What do they *do* that most other churches do not do?

WHAT EFFECTIVE APOSTOLIC CONGREGATIONS KNOW

1. People who aren't disciples are lost

Apostolic congregations know, as Samuel Shoemaker stressed, that people who are not following Jesus Christ and are not working out their salvation within the body of Christ are lost, and they cannot find the way to abundant life by themselves. They know this from Scripture, for our Lord revealed that such people are ''lost, like sheep without a shepherd.'' This revelation is confirmed as these churches observe contemporary society. As they observe the failing war against drugs, the rising tide of AIDS, the fragmentation of the family, the dry rot of the cities, the desperation of the underclass, the sweeping power of a dozen addictions, and the human stampede to cults and new religions, they see again that undiscipled people are lost and cannot find The Way by themselves. But the congregations also observe that many (declining) churches do not perceive that secular people are lost. Tragically, too many churches view the world through rose colored glasses; they mistake the masks that lost people wear for their real faces. Some churches even brand all people (and life-styles) as okay, and settle in with no mission at all. Apostolic churches are astonished by this myopia in the majority of churches, and they wonder ''what it would take'' for more churches to see the world through God's eyes.

2. Lost people matter to God

Since Adam and Eve's sin, lost people have mattered to God. Since the ancient promise to Abraham—that from his lineage all the families of the earth will be blessed—God has been moving in history to make a faith-relationship with God possible for all people. In the Great Commission, the Church is entrusted with the mandate to reach out to all people. Bill Hybels spotlights Luke 15, where Jesus links three parables together—stories of a lost sheep, a lost coin, and a lost son—and features their common threads: In each story, (1) something of great value is lost, (2) ''it matters so much that it warrants either an all-out search or an anguished vigil,'' and (3) when the sheep and coin are found and the son returns there is great ''rejoicing.''[30]

What's Jesus' message? That lost, wayward, rebellious, cursing people matter to God so much that He wants us to go after them. He wants us to search them out and bring them to Him.

Authentic evangelism flows from a mindset that acknowledges the ultimate value of people—forgotten people, lost people, wandering people, up-and-outers, down-and-outers—all people. The highest value is to love them, serve them, and reach them. Everything else goes up in smoke.

3. Church is primarily a mission to lost people, not primarily a gathered colony of the faithful

Rick Warren believes that, like Jesus, we must call ''not the righteous, but sinners, to repentance.'' Therefore, the local church's main business is not maintenance but mission; not nurturing Christians but discipling nonchristians. Indeed, the local church is *not* called to renew the existing church before reaching out, because the church's renewal begins *as* it obeys God by reaching out, and nothing renews the existing church like a steady stream of new believers. The church's identity is apostolic, so its main business is joining God in finding and loving lost people, and bringing them into the experiences, insights, faith, community, and mission that can set them free to become the people they were born to be and deeply yearn to be.

4. The importance of high expectations for their people

They know that high expectations for people are important because they know that nominal Christianity does not work, that nominal Christians are not yet fulfilled people experiencing the abundant life, that the world does not need a million more nominal Christians, and that nominal Christians do not advance, but rather frustrate, the christian movement in the world. They know, as Dean M. Kelley demonstrated in the early 1970s, that the truth claims of ''demanding'' churches are more believable.[31] Most seekers are not epistemologists competent to weigh every competing truth claim from astrology to Zen; so they tend to believe the movement whose people are giving, even sacrificing, the most for the movement. Seriousness suggests credibility and believability. So these churches expect all of their members to worship regularly, give generously, study the scriptures diligently, to open their souls to peers in a small group, to minister in accordance with their gifts, to witness for the faith in their social networks, to be in mission. They communicate that expectation to their people often, and they ''contract'' this with new members. But the expectations are not communicated as Law or duty, but rather as Grace and opportunity—the means by which we become God's powerful, compassionate, fulfilled, and reproductive people.

5. What to change and what to preserve

Churches growing in the West's mission fields seem to know what to change and what to preserve, whereas declining churches and denominations do not. For example, a pastor who had once tamed wild animals for a circus featured a lion and lamb—lying side by side, in a worship service. A denominational executive rebuked him, because such an approach to liturgy was not the denomination's "way!" If the pastor had preached some heresy, he would probably never have heard from the executive. The incident reveals a widespread confusion about content and form, what to be quick to change and what to be slow to change. I have observed that growing denominations are slow to change their theology and quick to change the cultural forms and styles in which they communicate their theology; declining denominations, however, are quick to change their theology and slow to change their forms and styles. Consequently, declining churches are experienced by secular people as both culturally anachronistic and lacking in deep consistent theological convictions.

Most churches reaching secular people stick to their theological roots; they know they are not likely to improve on "the faith once delivered to the saints." But they do accept the challenge to *meaningfully interpret* their tradition's theology to the unchurched. Because most unchurched people are not already enculturated into some ecclesiastical tradition, the interpretation often departs from the words and forms of the tradition and expresses the tradition's theological meaning in the words and forms of the host secular culture.

For example, as mentioned in chapter 2, Rick Warren preached a series of sermons at Saddleback Valley on what the christian tradition has called "the Seven Deadly Sins"—without ever referring to the series in those terms. He featured it as a series on "Breaking Free from the Habits and Hangups That Are Messing Up Your Life." The sermon on "Greed" addressed the question, "Why do I always feel like I have to have more?" The biblical answer is that "I think that *more* is going to bring me security, or satisfaction." But the biblical revelation confirms our experience that "having more" does not give us the security or satisfaction we seek, but knowing and following Christ can. Rick Warren even considers the biblical term *Lord*

147

negotiable, because it is not a term used in western culture today. He uses terms such as *leader* and *manager*. Warren says, "Jesus Christ wants to be the chairman of the board of your life," or "You need to make him the Chief Executive Officer in your life." He observes that a person in business understands, while the same person may not understand *Lord*. Warren's intention is *not* to change the theology but to use indigenous terms to get the faithful *meaning* across to secular people.

Rick Warren believes that this strategy is consistent with Paul's strategy that is explained in 1 Corinthians 9:20-22, in which Paul functions like a Jew to Jews and like a Gentile to Gentiles. "I have become all things to all people, that I might by all means save some." So, Warren explains, "I become like Saddleback Sam to win Saddleback Sam. I use his words, and his music, and I dress like he dresses and talk like he talks—in order to reach him." He believes that such a strategy does not compromise the message, but rather gives the message a fair chance! The message is unchanging, but the forms and methods vary. Furthermore, what works today may not work tomorrow, because the people and culture around the church are constantly changing. Such a policy for the church implies a willingness to change, and "to operate out of your comfort zone." Unfortunately, most churches simply perpetuate the kind of church they are comfortable with. "Too many churches operate just like they did 25 years ago!"

6. The importance of understanding, loving, and liking secular people

Rick Warren and Bill Hybels both learned, from Robert Schuller, that the communicator must learn to "think like a nonchristian." While many Christians live too much like nonchristians, they don't think like secular people think. The longer you are a believer, the less you think like an unbeliever; and if you think like a pastor, you are two steps removed from the unchurched mind! Rick Warren exhibits the problem through an analogy: We are broadcasting on CB channel 9, but they are listening on channel 13, "so no matter how good the message is, its not getting through. You have to get on their level," and begin with their agenda. Warren reports that he meets very few lost people who are asking questions about the doctrine of transubstantiation, or the inspiration of the Bible. He says that our church people want their church to be more relevant to the style and conscious concerns of unchurched people, because they want a church they would be comfortable inviting their friends to visit.

But, how do we learn how secular people think? Rick Warren found that it's as simple as talking to them, spending time with them, and asking them questions. He believes that "asking the right questions leads to the right answers, which leads to the right strategy, which leads to the right results." Warren asked about 500 people not currently involved in any church four questions:

1. "What do you think is the greatest need in our area?" Half of what they say will involve issues the church cannot do anything about, like high prices. Your objective is to get them to talking about personal issues.
2. "Why do you think most people don't attend church?" Phrased this way, the question puts them on the majority side and undefensive, and they are free to give you *their* reason.
3. "If you were looking for a church, what kind of things would you look for?" You discover that what they would look for is *not* what most churches are offering, though they *could*.
4. "What advice would you give me? How can our church help you?" Unchurched people have heard churches say, "Come help us," but not, "How can we help you?"

Warren suggests that the communicator's big challenge is to choose to learn to think as nonchristians do. Once the communicator makes that decision, the skill increases over time.

Warren's survey revealed four reasons why unchurched people don't attend: (1) Sermons are boring, and irrelevant to their lives. (2) The members are unfriendly to visitors. (3) Churches seem more interested in your money than in you as a person. (4) They want quality child care if they go to church. He noticed that these reasons are not theological reasons, but "sociological hangups" with the church. So Warren changed his preaching style, coached his people in welcoming behaviors, played down money, organized exquisite child care, and marketed Saddleback Valley Community Church as "a church for people who have given up on traditional worship services."

Bill Hybels has learned that understanding the way secular people think is the first of two absolute prerequisites to reaching them. This understanding can be achieved by making friends with nonchristians and by sharing some authentic interest area in their lives—such as a sport. Many pastors, and other Christians, will resist this suggestion, because it may mean moving out of their comfort zone. But. according to Hybels, "we can't win them if we don't know how they think, and we can't know how they think if we don't ever enter their world."[32]

Bill Hybels's second prerequisite to reaching secular people is loving and liking them. If we don't, they can sense it; if we do, it makes engagement possible. We learn to love and like them them by focusing on their needs. When Hybels first entered the ministry, he was so impressed by unchurched people's appearance, attire, homes, and cars that he wondered whether they really needed church.

> The longer I worked with them, though, the more I realized, these people have gaping holes in their lives. That pretty wife hasn't slept with her husband in three months. Those kids, if you could ever get close to them, are so mad at their dad they'd fill your ears. That home is mortgaged to the hilt, and that job that looks so sweet isn't all that secure. That guy who looks so confident is scared stiff inside.
> That appearance of sufficiency is a thin veneer, and underneath is a boatload of need that we . . . are equipped and called to address in the power of the Holy Spirit.[33]

Hybels now knows that secular people "are like sheep without a shepherd, and [that] we have got the Shepherd to offer them. So lets get together and try to get them connected before its too late."

7. *The importance of accepting unchurched people*

Churches that reach secular people seem consciously to begin where people are, rather than insist that people be where the church would like them to be. They know that God once accepted us as we were, and that the church is called to reflect God's own posture toward sinners with accepting compassion. But how does a church with high moral standards, and high expectations for its people, maintain both high expectations for its people and non-judgmental acceptance of nonchristians? Rick Warren explains that any church wanting to minister to unchurched people must not be "easily shocked" if their life-styles vary from Christian norms. He explains that a church can be sufficiently ''shock proof'' if it simply ''does not expect an unbeliever to act like a believer until he or she is one.'' Unfortunately, many churches do not project an attitude of acceptance because they ''confuse acceptance with approval.'' It is possible, however, to accept someone without approving their life-style, and such acceptance is a prerequisite for their consideration of a new life-style.

8. The importance of using music that secular people understand

Rick Warren discovered that to reach secular people the church ''must use words they understand, and music they understand also.'' Saddleback Valley Community Church does not feature classical music because classical music accounts for only 2 percent of the album sales in the United States. Warren explains, ''Some 90 percent of album sales are contemporary music, so in our church's music ministry we are 'unabashedly contemporary.' '' More specifically, the church tends to use the particular genres of music that are most heard on the radio stations by their target population. Rick Warren elaborated on the importance of music in my interview with him:

In my opinion, music is the most important factor in determining your evangelistic target, even more than preaching style. Because there are many different age groups and economic levels that will listen to my message if it is personal, practical, positive, if it applies to their life, and if I speak it with sincerity and integrity, and in a down-to-earth not-an-oratory style and voice.

But when you choose your music, you are determining exactly who you are going to reach and who you are not going to reach. More than any other factor, tell me what the music is in a church, and I will tell you who that church will be able to reach and who they will never be able to reach.

Saddleback Valley Church's implementation of this philosophy of indigenous music is instructive. Warren explains that ''we don't have an organ; we never will. We don't have a choir; never will. We don't have a piano; never will.'' They do have a contemporary orchestra, with a string section, brass section, drums, and electronic synthesizer. And they have many soloists, and singing groups—from duets to ensembles—each smaller than a choir; and each singer sings with an individual microphone—"because that is the kind of sound people's ears are accustomed to."

The music mix in other churches reaching secular people varies from Saddleback Church, in part because their target populations vary. Most churches reaching secular people do have a piano—often a grand piano. They are much less likely to feature an organ—though the Crystal Cathedral features a pipe organ. The Church on Brady, a multiethnic urban neighborhood Southern Baptist church in East Los Angeles, features a grand piano, an electronic synthesizer, an electric guitar, drums, an eight-piece band, and a half dozen singing groups in a moving forty-minute music celebration that launches each ninety-minute worship service. The Church on Brady, apparently, owns no hymnals; all congregational singing uses overhead projectors beaming each song's words on front walls.

Some churches targeting unchurched people do very well with less instrumentation. The new electronic synthesizers present such an astonishing range of musical sound that some new congregations use that exclusively. In Lexington, Kentucky, the new Crossroads Christian Church, with less than three years of history, is approaching 300 average attendance. Their stirring contemporary services feature piano, synthesizer, and taped soundtracks. Virtually any attire seems appropriate for the service at Crossroads, and coffee and donuts are served at the back of the sanctuary throughout the service.

Willow Creek Community Church features a block of contemporary music in its weekend "seekers services," with a grand piano and a large orchestra. They also feature a skit in each service—which dramatizes the theme for the service and enables the seeker to identify with a character. They believe drama has become a necessary medium to reach the first generation which grew up on TV sitcoms. According to pastor Bill Hybels, "They have to see it, and not just hear about it, to process the value being discussed."

Willow Creek's investment in contemporary music and drama strategically avoids the usual overreliance on the preached word, and follows an intentionally redundant strategy for communicating the gospel: (1) They believe in the revelatory value of multiple conversations between seekers and Christians in the secular world. (2) They schedule small group meetings and large forums in which seekers can dialogue and ask questions. Then, in the weekend worship services, they rely on (3) music, (4) drama, and (5) the preached gospel—largely in that order, because, as Bill Hybels explains: "A person's resistance to persuasion is very high when spoken to, but very low when exposed to drama and music."[34] (6) Willow Creek relies also on tapes and books in their redundant communication strategy. People can buy, for $2.00, a tape of the message they just heard as they leave the service, and Willow Creek's bookstore features books relating to that day's topic.

9. The importance of starting new congregations

Rick Warren knows that no one church can win all the unchurched people; it takes many kinds of churches to win many kinds of people. He says, "We believe the key to the Great Commission is starting new churches, [because] new churches grow faster than old churches." He perceives that the port of entry for most seekers is a worship service. Some churches can reform their liturgy and music to be seeker sensitive or can start new alternative worship services. But Warren suggests that if most churches instituted in their traditional service what it takes to reach unbelievers, a revolution would occur! He advocates starting many new churches—while reforming as many existing churches as possible. Challenge existing churches "to birth new churches for a new generation." The Saddleback Valley Community Church is modeling this Great Commission. In the first ten years of its history, the church started fourteen daughter congregations.

Other bellwether churches take varying approaches to new church planting. The Church on Brady has in recent years started five new congregations in Southern California and ten in other countries—including four in the Philippines and three in Mexico City. The Brady leaders now project starting new congregations in seven different countries within a year. Willow Creek is not as noted as some great churches for planting daughter congregations, but their three pastors conferences per year teach their model and rationale to about 1,500 pastors. *Time* magazine reported that "dozens of copycat congregations have begun popping up around the country."[35]

10. The importance of involvement in world mission

The apostolic congregation's concern to reach people is not limited to the people in its ministry area; through world mission, they reach out to other peoples of other lands and cultures. They support their denomination's mission program, but that is just the beginning. They also support their own missionaries, and their own mission programs. And they involve great numbers of their own people in short-term ventures in mission—working in immunization clinics, digging wells, planting churches, and a range of other specific activities that do some good, change people's lives, and help them to "own" Christianity's world mission. In 1980 when Rick Warren preached his first sermon for the Saddleback Community Church, he shared the vision "of sending out hundreds of career missionaries and church workers all around the world, and sending out our members by the thousands on short-term mission projects to every continent." He believes that sending people on mission profoundly affects the growth of the *sending* congregation, as well as the growth of the Church in other lands. "Churches grow not just on their seating capacity, but also on their sending capacity." An increasing number of other churches are discovering this same synergism. For instance, The Church on Brady has over 100 members preparing for mission vocations.

WHAT EFFECTIVE APOSTOLIC CONGREGATIONS DO

1. Research the community and the unchurched population

Rick Warren believes that there is no substitute for becoming an expert on your community. He says, "The pastor ought to know more about that community than anybody else. . . . You cannot reach people unless you understand them first." This means discovering who lives there, and why; what they think, and act like; what they like and dislike. Reading the local newspaper, and the journal *American*

Demographics, and books like Arnold Mitchell's *The Nine American Lifestyles* can help, as can interviews with school principals, marketing people, regional planning people, and leaders of the community's human services. But, Warren believes, nothing takes the place of interviewing 200 or more unchurched people.

When Willow Creek church was started in 1975, several leaders went door to door for several months, asking questions that helped them gain a working knowledge of adult non-churched persons in their region of metropolitan Chicago. The two most frequent reasons for not going to church were similar to those cited in Warren's surveys in Southern California: (1) They saw no relevance of the church to their lives, no connections between church and their daily life, work, family, and relationships. So church was perceived as "a waste of time." (2) They saw churches as only interested in money; that is all they care about.[36]

2. "Profile" their target population

After researching the community and the unchurched population, the apostolic church develops a cogent demographic profile of the unchurched population they are called to reach. An informed profile helps inform many strategic decisions the church must make. Robert Schuller's rationale for such a profile has been widely influential: "Their *needs* determine our *programs*. Their *hangups* determine our *strategy*. Their *culture* determines our *style*. Their *population* determines our *goals*."[37]

Saddleback Valley Community Church developed the following profile of "Saddleback Sam":

"Saddleback Sam" is a well educated young urban professional. He is self-satisfied, and comfortable with his life. He likes his job and where he lives. He is affluent, recreation conscious, and prefers the casual and informal over the formal. He is interested in health and fitness, and he thinks he is enjoying life more than 5 years ago, but he is overextended in time and money, and is stressed out. He has some religious background from childhood, but he hasn't been to church for 15 or 20 years, and he is skeptical of "organized religion." He doesn't want to be recognized when he comes to church.

Willow Creek's profiles of "Unchurched Harry" and ("Unchurched Mary") have not been summarized as compactly, but the church's leaders are of one mind on who they intend to reach: (1) The target is male, reasoning that if they designed a service males would appreciate, they might reach the whole family. (2) The target population is 25 or 30 to 50 years of age, (3) and college educated, white collar, with some blue collar foreman types. (4) Many are entrepreneurial self-starter types. (5) Most have some church in their background, so they would know who Moses is, but they do not really know much of Christianity and its gospel; they are unchurched now and have been for years. (6) If they did try church, they would look for things like creativity and variety, applicability to life, male and female leadership, anonymity for themselves, and no pressure; "they don't want to sing anything, sign anything, say anything, or give anything." So the Willow Creek leaders decided "to provide a safe place for seekers to consider the dangerous message of Jesus Christ." When I asked Bill Hybels "What are the main characteristics of secular unchurched people that the christian evangelist most needs to keep in mind?" his ready answer indicated how clearly Willow Creek's leaders know the people they are reaching:

> The baby boom generation in our area is slowly realizing that the meeting of their material needs is not going to satisfy the yearnings of their souls.
>
> They are finding out that relationships that they thought were going to have a fairy tale ending are not turning out that way. Their relational worlds are falling apart at the seams. They don't know where to turn and what to do about it, but it's all very confusing and disconcerting for them.
>
> Many are reaching mid-life and asking themselves "What is it all about? Am I going to live the next 30 or 40 years of my life the way I have lived the first half? There has got to be more to life than achievement, and going through the motions of my job, and a football game on weekends. I mean, there's got to be more."

3. Define a clear mission and plan for the future

In my interview with Bill Hybels, I asked him, "How do most churches need to change to reach unchurched secular people?" He commented that very few churches have any idea what they are doing. They don't know what their objectives are, what their overall purposes are, and whether or not they are achieving them. So, it's just a weekly rehash of things that were done last year, and the year before—with no sense of direction, or achievable goals, so that the congregation can say, "We are making progress."

By contrast, the growing churches who disciple secular people have a clear defining purpose. They know what "business" they are in. They are clear about why they exist. Their apostolic or missional identity is clear, rehearsed, and reinforced. Their purpose is usually expressed in a mission statement, such as Saddleback Valley's: "A Great Commitment to the Great Commandment and the Great Commission Will Produce a Great Church."

Saddleback Valley's mission statement helps them clarify their priorities. The Great Commandment to love God mandates *worship*; the commandment to love the neighbor mandates *ministry*; the Great Commission to "go . . . make disciples" mandates *evangelism*; and the commission to "teach them to observe all that I have commanded you" mandates *discipleship*. The church thus majors on these four basics, to the extent that if a program or activity does not fit one of those priorities, they are not interested in doing it. These four mandates are fleshed out in four purpose statements:

1. We exist to celebrate God's presence in worship.
2. We exist to communicate God's message in evangelism.
3. We exist to educate God's people in discipleship.
4. We exist to demonstrate God's love in ministry.

Rick Warren believes that the leader's first responsibility is to clarify and communicate the purposes of the church. The mission and purposes are usually worked out collaboratively with the people, but it is the leader's job to communicate, often and redundantly, the church's vision, mission, and purposes. When the church's people are clear about the church's main business, that mission drives the church.

With their main business, mission, and purposes clear, these churches then develop a long-range strategic plan for achieving their purposes. The strategic plan is developed collaboratively, so that the plan will have widespread ownership. Its flow typically runs from the general to the specifics, that is, from mission statement, to objectives, to strategies, to programs and activities, to the operational plans for each program and activity. Periodically, the church will take a fresh reading of its strengths and environment, and modify the strategic plan accordingly.[38]

4. Develop and implement a strategy for reaching unchurched people

Apostolic churches also develop a specific strategy for reaching the unchurched people in their ministry area. Willow Creek's strategy is an outstanding case.[39] They developed the strategy as they reflected upon one paramount question: "How can we get Unchurched Harry from where he is, to meet Christ, to become a disciple, to become mature in Christ?" A "Seven-Step Strategy" resulted:

1. Some believer will have to build a relationship with Unchurched Harry. Harry is likely insulated from the influence of Christianity, so a Christian will develop a credible, integrity-filled relationship with Harry.
2. As the Holy Spirit gives opportunity, the Christian gives a verbal witness of the gospel to Harry, which focuses Harry's thinking and shapes several (or more) conversations over time.
3. The Christian brings Harry to some weekend services for seekers at Willow Creek Church, which begins to involve the whole church in Harry's evangelization. Harry works through the christian possibility without any pressure, at his own pace.
4. When Harry becomes a Christian, he is invited (usually brought) to the New Community service for believers, which meets on Wednesday or Thursday night. This service involves Harry in corporate worship, Bible exposition, communion and large-scale fellowship, and helps integrate him into the Body of Christ.
5. In this same season, Harry joins a small group where, in close fellowship, he experiences encouragement, prayer support, and accountability.
6. In this same season, Harry becomes involved in some service or ministry that is consistent with his personality and spiritual gifts for ministry.
7. Harry becomes a steward of his time and talent, he now works to advance the Kingdom, and he befriends "Unchurched Larry"—in whom the seven steps are repeated.

5. Deploy their laity in ministry

The biggest challenge and opportunity facing most churches, Rick Warren believes, is "to turn an audience into an army." In

Saddleback Valley Church, "the people are the ministers, and the pastors are the 'administers.' " The proper role of pastors is to "lead and feed" the laity, and otherwise prepare and equip them for their mission in the world. In most churches, unfortunately, the opposite pattern prevails: the pastor tries to (and is expected to) do all the ministry, while the laity make the decisions, administer the church through many committees, and evaluate the pastor's ministry performance. This is a non-growth model, because the pastor cannot care for more than about 200 people. For the church to become a movement in the community, the ministry has to be released into the body of believers—with leadership in the hands of the few, and ministry in the hands of the many.

In time, the laity become an entrepreneurial people, as ideas for new ministries are generated more and more from turned-on, experienced laity. Saddleback Valley encourages, and challenges, its people to seek opportunities for ministry. One fellow started a "Maintenance Ministry"—in which he, and several other men, now fix cars for widows and single women. Another man launched "Home Helps," and now a cadre of people do volunteer carpentry repairs in homes.

An increasing number of churches across North America are encouraging an entrepreneurial laity. A layman in The Church on Brady, in East Los Angeles, started a street counseling ministry in front of an abortion clinic—which has rescued about 150 babies in a three-year period. A young woman, having become a Christian through an addiction recovery ministry, started "Clean and Sober"—a ministry to addicted people in 12-Step groups who have not yet committed their lives to Christ.

At Frazer Memorial United Methodist Church, in Montgomery, Alabama, a layperson heard of several expectant couples who learned their baby was to be born with a deformity or handicap. The church started a support group for these couples. When their babies were born, this led naturally to another support group for parents with such babies or children. This led to the equipping and staffing of a special nursery for these children during worship services and church programs. Today, the church helps relieve stress in the lives of these parents by staffing the nursery for "Friday Night Out" every week. These ministries, and several others, for these children and their parents are now in operation. Every such ministry was conceived by a layperson, and is led and staffed by laypersons.

How do these churches know what ministry is appropriate for a given layperson? The trend in bellwether churches seems to be against recruiting people for roles and tasks. John Ed Mathison, Senior Pastor of Frazer Memorial, observed that many people will comply when you recruit them for a job, but then give the task less than their best energy. Most people give priority energy to tasks they volunteer for, and therefore "own." So Frazer Memorial, each Fall, gives people a "menu" of 150 options for involvement in ministry. The norm is for every member to prayerfully choose one ministry, for which they will be oriented and trained in January, in which they will serve for that year. New members are given the same menu, and involvement in a ministry is part of the "contract" when they join.[40]

Willow Creek's approach to placing people is consistent with Frazer's. Each new member completes a four-week "Network Seminar" that helps them discover their spiritual gifts for ministry. A lay counselor then helps them find the several options for ministry that fit both their personality type and their spiritual gifts, and asks which one they most have a passion for.

6. Train their people for christian witness

The christian movement today has such a prepared and able generation of laity for fulfilling the Great Commission that most pastors simply challenge the people and turn them loose. That ought to work, but it seldom does. Ken Chafin observes:

We have . . . tended to underestimate the average lay person's need for some specific training in the sharing of his faith. This is an area in which I have had to "eat crow." For years I believed that any person who was a Christian could use the skills he already had to witness. I was wrong.

I watched women who had drive and ingenuity enough to make them excellent presidents of the PTA who were unable to tell the children in their class how to become Christians. I watched lawyers who were qualified to try cases before the Supreme Court who could not sit down in the living room of an interested friend and present a good "brief" for Jesus Christ. While there are certain carryovers that relate to insights and attitudes, I've discovered that most of the best people in the church need some help in learning to communicate their faith.[41]

How do bellwether churches train their laity for witness? Willow Creek's "Impact Evangelism Seminar" for laity serves as a good model. The seminar, which is led by two staff, meets two and a half hours one evening per week for four weeks. Their approach is distinctive in three respects: (1) it gives people options, (2) it encourages people to be themselves, (3) and it prepares Christians for an apologetic role—that is, to respond with good reasons to questions and doubts.

The first session, "Being Yourself," informs people that you don't have to be odd or great to do evangelism, and there is no "one approach" prescribed in Scripture. Indeed, Scripture models at least a half dozen ways to reach people.[42] A *confrontational* approach is modeled by Peter, in Acts 2, as he openly declares the good news that "God has made this Jesus, whom you crucified, both Lord and Christ," and invites people to "repent and be baptized." A more *intellectual* approach is modeled by Paul, in Acts 17, as Paul establishes some common ground with the people by referring to their altar "to an unknown God," by sharing that he has come to represent that God, and by engaging the Jews and God-fearing Greeks with reasons and explanations that help them understand this new message. A *testimonial* approach is reflected in John 9, when the blind beggar whom Jesus healed began telling the story of what happened to him. A *relational* approach is mandated in Mark 5. Jesus, after exorcising the demons from a possessed man, directed the man to "go home" and share what God is doing with his family and friends. An *invitational* approach is modeled in John 4 where the Samaritan woman, who has concluded that Jesus must be the Messiah, invites the people to come see and hear Jesus for themselves. A *serving* approach is modeled, in Acts 9, by the woman Dorcas—who made clothing for poor people, gave them away in the name of Christ, and thereby pointed people to a compassionate God. The purpose of this session is to give options to Christians and to demonstrate that people who cannot be won by one method may be won by another method that is more appropriate to them.

The second session, "Telling Your Story," teaches ways to start spiritual conversations and prepares participants to share their personal testimony—without using christian jargon.

The third session, "Making the Message Clear," teaches people four or five ways to make the gospel clear through analogies, illustrations, and stories.

The fourth session, "Answering Questions," helps prepare people for the apologetic role required in evangelism in a secular society, and gives them resources to turn to when people have questions.[43] Beyond the apologetics session of the Impact Evangelism Seminar, Willow Creek works at the ministry of apologetics—that is, giving good reasons and evidence to seekers—more than any other church I am familiar with. A tear-off part of each week's bulletin gives seekers a chance to request a conversation. The church provides one-on-one conversations for seekers to raise their questions. The much larger weekly "Foundations Class" for seekers provides a large forum to address their questions. Occasionally, a New Community (midweek) service is devoted to a panel on "Questions Skeptics Ask." After the panel speaks, people in the congregation contribute their insights, so the church is constantly expanding its capacity to converse with seekers. The church's bookword store features books and tapes that prepare Christians for this dimension of evangelistic sharing, and other books and tapes for seekers asking questions.

Lee Strobel, a former athiest who came to Christ through Willow Creek and is now its director of communication. He clarifies the modest but necessary role that apologetics plays in Willow Creek's evangelism ministries: Many secular seekers have had experiences with Christians whose faith does not have a conscious factual foundation—who cannot articulate reasons in support of what they believe. Furthermore, most seekers have heard the secular rumor that Christianity doesn't have sufficient facts, evidence, and reason on its side; they think faith is "blind faith." Strobel explains:

Frequently, when you share with someone about Christ, they have one question that has always bothered them, and it's been a barrier. So, if I can say—"That's a good question, and I used to wonder about that too; here is what I found out"—that helps them. A good answer, even if less than completely satisfying, frees them up to go five or six steps. They may not even have a second question.

In Willow Creek's approach to apologetics, the Christian is not the seeker's adversary—trying to beat Unchurched Harry or Mary with superior argumentation. The Christian is the seeker's ally—helping, for as long as necessary, to work through doubts and hangups for the step of faith to become possible. Willow Creek's leaders are clear that the best of reasons establish only probability in a person's mind. "No one can say 'Jesus is Lord' except by the Holy Spirit." In any case, most seekers do not need *all* doubts dispelled before they come to faith; they mainly need to know that good reasons do exist in support of christian truth claims. In western culture's split between a "public world of facts" and a "private world of values," secular people assume that no option within the private realm is factual. But Christianity— as God's revelation in history, does have a factual basis, and some of the facts are attainable. As Lee Strobel discovered during his search, "Jesus was in history. He left footprints that can be checked out!"

Willow Creek's leaders are committed to giving Unchurched Harry and Mary sufficient unpressured time to come to terms with the offer to become a disciple, but they are not passive about Harry and Mary's response to Christ. They encourage him or her to come to terms with Christ's invitation in measurable time, and the average seeker takes about six to twelve months to reach this decision. Willow Creek does employ one special strategy to help people along, consistent with the "trial" stage of the adoption process and the "experiment of faith" from the Shoemaker legacy. Seekers are encouraged to begin applying the wisdom of Scripture to some specific area of their lives—such as their marriage, parenting, or work—for a season, and start acting as though the Scripture is true. Willow Creek's objectives in this penultimate form of invitation seem to be twofold. (1) The first objective is to cooperate with that psychologically necessary "trial" stage in the adoption process. On important life-determining matters, most people cannot leap from interest to adoption without going through a trial, or experimental, period. (2) The second objective is to increase the seeker's respect for the authority of Scripture. Hybels explains:

Unchurched people don't give the Bible a fraction of the weight we believers do. They look at it as an occasionally useful collection of helpful suggestions, something like the Farmer's Almanac. They tend to think, "The Bible has some neat things to say once in a while, but we all know it's not the kind of thing I'm going to change my life radically to obey."[44]

The experiment of faith—applying Scripture's wisdom to one area of life for a season—is usually self-authenticating, and seekers infer that since they can trust the wisdom of Scripture, maybe they can trust God!

7. Offer a "seeker sensitive" Sunday worship service

In 1979, Lee Strobel's wife became a Christian at Willow Creek, and she invited him to visit the church. Lee, a journalist with legal training, and legal affairs editor of *The Chicago Tribune,* professed atheism because he wanted more evidence. He observed, however, great positive changes in his wife; once shy, for instance, her faith brought her out of her shell. So Lee agreed to attend a service with her. He was astonished by the degree to which the service ''seemed to hit me where I was at.'' He felt completely comfortable in the theater where the church then held services. The music sounded similar to what he listened to on the radio. The drama was effective in raising issues—without offering simplistic solutions. And Bill Hybels's message spoke about matters Lee could relate to, and even used illustrations out of motorcycling—which Lee liked to do. ''The relevance struck me—that church could be relevant, that it could have implications for my life today.'' Furthermore, they seemed to respect him, they took his questions seriously, they responded nondefensively and nonjudgmentally, and they didn't pressure him—but gave him time to investigate and reflect at his own pace. Strobel felt like the service ''was designed just for me.'' Later, he found out it was designed just for him! ''I was their exact target audience. In effect, they had constructed a service which was directed exactly at me—I fit the profile of 'Unchurched Harry.' ''

The other major influence upon Lee Strobel was the transparent credibility of the people he observed and interacted with, people with whom he identified.

Another thing that struck me is—''They believe this stuff!'' A lot of so-called Christians I had met through my life had mouthed some things, or did some things on Sunday—but I never saw it evidenced in who they were or how they acted.

But at Willow Creek I saw people who really believed it! And these were *normal* people—people who I would like to hang around with. They were appealing people, who didn't put on airs and didn't set themselves up as holier-than-thou. I could identify with them, and they had a story to tell from their hearts that they were convinced of, and it was enough to convince me that I at least ought to look into it.

In addition to the rightness of the service on that first visit, Bill Hybels's message influenced Strobel. The message enabled Strobel to make sense of the concept of *grace* for the first time, and Strobel reacted inwardly: ''I don't believe it! It's too good to be true! But if it is true, it has tremendous implications for my life.'' For almost two years, Strobel investigated the Scriptures, archaeological evidence, other religions, and ''a series of puzzle pieces were being put together.''

Strobel's quest was not merely philosophical but also experimental. He began applying Scripture's wisdom to his marriage, and his marriage got better! One day, he realized that enough of the pieces were in place to warrant becoming a Christian.

Then I didn't know what to do. My wife said, ''Here is a verse you might want to read,'' and she handed me John 1:12—''To as many as received him, to them he gave power to become children of God, even to them who believe in his name.'' So I realized it's not enough just to know it; I had to do something with it. That's when I committed my life to Christ. I had heard, often, at Willow Creek about the necessity of commitment, but it had to be reiterated to me. At that point I had to be taken by the hand, with someone saying, ''This is your next step.''

A new life began for Lee Strobel when he attended that first ''seeker sensitive'' weekend service at Willow Creek, though other experiences contributed to his spiritual growth.

Bill Hybels learned to design events to reach secular people like Strobel while leading the youth ministry for a church in the Chicago area. He, with his christian kids, designed an evening for their non-christian friends. They refurbished the room, put up posters and banners, featured contemporary music, a multi-media presentation, and a drama—in which nonchurched kids saw themselves. And Hybels shifted from his customary expository Bible studies to a topical approach with insights from the Scriptures and applications for life.

That formula, with refinement, serves Willow Creek Church to this day, and their considerable experience stands behind their most important strategic principle: "That you cannot do evangelism and edification optimally at the same time, in the same place, in the same meeting." They discovered that, in a service trying to do both, if you focus a service for believers, the visiting seekers feel left out and that Christianity doesn't apply to them. If you focus on the seekers, the believers who need the "meat" of Scripture will feel like they are malnourished inside. If you shoot for the middle, you miss both populations.

So they decided to devote the Sunday morning service to engaging seekers, and thereby take advantage of the norm still present in western culture—that if your life gets bad enough, and you have tried everything else, you might try God on a Sunday! They also started the New Community service, for believers, on Wednesday nights. Willow Creek now holds three weekend services for seekers, Saturday evening at 6:00 and Sunday morning at 9:00 and 11:00, serving over 14,000 attenders per weekend. They also hold two New Community services each week, Wednesday and Thursday evenings at 7:30, serving over 6,000 believers—over 70 percent of whom became Christians through the Willow Creek ministry.

Willow Creek's major facility resembles a convention center more than a traditional church. The people sit in theater seats facing a stage. The building has no stained glass or other traditional christian symbols. The auditorium was designed for excellent sound and lighting. The service moves with almost a choreographed professionalism. Hybels speaks from behind a plexiglass lectern. As one leaves the service, booths throughout the lobby feature opportunities to sign up for one or another of the church's ministries.

The service typically features an orchestra, several singing groups and vocalists, contemporary music, a multi-media presentation, and a five- to seven-minute dramatic sketch. Then Hybels addresses, from the Scriptures, a seeker-relevant topic—like "Fanning the Flames of Marriage," or "Facing Up to Fear," "Getting a Grip on Life," or "A Whole New You"—with human interest, life applications, and humor. In one message Hybels put in a good word for sex: "Think how boring life would be without sexuality. There'd be no country-western music, no swimsuit edition of *Sports Illustrated*, and Madonna would be unemployed!" The content of the whole service presupposes that the target audience knows nothing, so the message is basic "Christianity 101."

166

Willow Creek's approach is based on their research of the unchurched populations of metropolitan Chicago, and on the resulting profile of "Unchurched Harry." Their research told them that if Harry decides to visit a church he wants: (1) anonymity: he wants to be left alone to look it over, he doesn't want to say anything, or sign anything, or be "recognized." (2) Harry wants things to happen at an introductory level—so he can understand. (3) He wants relevance. It has to make a difference to his life situation, or he will conclude that "Christianity doesn't relate to my life," so Hybels especially wants his "messages" (not "sermons") to have "high user-take-home-value." (4) Harry's enculturation in the professional world of Chicago primes him to expect "excellence" from a church service he is willing to take seriously; if it is "bush league" he will write it off. (5) Harry wants time to decide—with respect for his questions, without pressure to make up his mind.[45] According to Hybels, most conversions occur

after people have attended the church for six months or more. The secular person has to attend consistently for half a year and have the person who brought him witness to him the whole time. He needs that much time simply to kick the tires, look at the interior, and check the title before he can finally say, "I'll buy it."

So Willow Creek adapts to its market, hoping to remove the "cultural barrier" between the traditional church and secular people. They want their people to be so excited about the service for seekers that they will want to invite their friends to attend it—with no reservations, inhibitions, or embarrassment. Hybels says that the service's objective is to engage

that seeker who is trying to find meaning in life and answers to perplexing ethical questions. And since Unchurched Harry can be downright hostile to organized religion and doesn't expect to find any answers in church, the goal of the weekend services at Willow Creek is to break down his defenses and get him to give religion another chance.[46]

8. Challenge people to commit their lives

In the target model for making Christians, secular seekers cross image, cultural, and gospel barriers to become Christians and then a "total devotion" barrier to become fulfilled Christians who are useful to the movement. While some churches ignore the fourth barrier and avoid extending the "life commitment" challenge, churches like Willow Creek are not content to leave people as mere "Christians," because God requires and the world demands that Christians be totally devoted to God's Kingdom and because the deepest needs of their own souls will not otherwise be met. Bill Hybels's observation about this challenge warrants repeating: "becoming totally devoted to Christ" is the most difficult single topic to get across to people.[47] "When I teach that to secularly minded people, they think I'm from Mars. The thought of living according to someone else's agenda is ludicrous"; it contradicts western culture's myth that "you can have it all."[48]

Hybels offers some helpful suggestions for fulfilling this awesome communication challenge: (1) Describe total commitment from the specifics of Scripture—like loving God, loving your neighbor and even your enemy, seeking first the Kingdom of God, and dying daily to self-will. (2) Challenge the congregation's leaders to model the totally committed lifestyle; then it becomes a more engaging and contagious idea. (3) Preach and teach commitment within the framework of many different topics. (4) Expose the alternatives to wholehearted commitment; "play out the opposite scenario." Hybels gives us a memorable example:

All he ever really wanted in life was more. He wanted more money, so he parlayed inherited wealth into a billion-dollar pile of assets. He wanted more fame, so he broke into the Hollywood scene and soon became a filmmaker and star. He wanted more sensual pleasures, so he paid handsome sums to indulge his every sexual urge. He wanted more thrills, so he designed, built, and piloted the fastest aircraft in the world. He wanted more power, so he secretly dealt political favors so skillfully that two U. S. presidents became his pawns. All he ever wanted was more. He was absolutely convinced that more would bring him true satisfaction.

[But] this man concluded his life—emaciated; colorless; sunken chest; fingernails in grotesque, inches-long corkscrews; rotting, black teeth; tumors; innumerable needle marks from his drug addiction. Howard Hughes died . . . believing the myth of more. He died a billionaire junkie, insane by all reasonable standards.[49]

Hybels also recommends that we "patiently let the Spirit work" in the souls of our people. All believers are called to "abandon themselves to full commitment to Christ,'' but ''becoming wholly devoted is a process'' and ''all believers cannot do that at the same pace.'' We keep the challenge before them as good news, and we trust the Holy Spirit to do God's work. Total surrender and a new, empowered, altruistic life cannot come by human effort alone, but only by an additional work of grace in a person's heart. Believers are called to seek that second work of grace with all their hearts, and to live with the expectation that God will indeed sanctify them, and make them all they were created to be, in this life.

9. *Open their hearts to the presence and power of God*

The churches that reach secular people in today's western mission fields are not ''god-evaders'' who, like some churches in cultural captivity, use their rituals, routines, meetings, activities, and ''good church work'' to keep God at a distance. Apostolic congregations want all of God they can get; they are a Holy Spirit people. They want any gifts that the Holy Spirit has in mind, and any assignments that the Holy Spirit has in mind. They yearn to become, and expect to become, the people they were born to be—in this life. The Spirit sometimes uses this window of openness to visit and bless God's people; sometimes they see at the time that God is with them, more often through a rear view mirror. And because of their credibility and God-consciousness, seekers are able to sense the presence of the Spirit in their midst.

10. *Want other churches to join them in reaching out to secular people*

The secular nations and populations of the western world represent vast mission fields, receptive winnable mission fields—for churches willing to affirm their apostolic role and begin, culturally, where people are. Some church leaders have known this for decades, and yet it is still hard to find churches whose prime mission is to find and reconcile lost people. Churches like the Crystal Cathedral, University Presbyterian Church in Seattle, Walnut Street Baptist Church in Louisville, St. Luke's United Methodist Church in

Orlando, Florida, First Church of Christ in Wethersfield, Connecticut, Frazer Memorial United Methodist Church in Montgomery, The Church on Brady in East Los Angeles, Saddleback Valley, Willow Creek, and other churches cited in this book are still regarded as "exceptional"—as though maintenance and chaplaincy were the biblical norm! There still aren't many apostolic experiments in the modern West.

Bill Hybels and I reflected on why this is the case. We were able to identify three reasons. First, it is hard work to fashion a church for the unchurched, the waters are not clearly charted, and the leader risks failure. It is much easier to develop a church for people already convinced, and do church work as we always have, and grow by transfer growth, and love each other, and prepare to go to heaven together.

Second, Christians, as a group, are more lovable than pagans, and ordained ministers get more respect, strokes, and love from the faithful; but secular unchurched people have no reason to respect a pastor's vocation or take a pastor seriously.

Third, there are larger dynamics involved in apostolic work. Hybels said:

> When we decide to invade enemy territory, and befriend people on the other side of the line, and to take the risks of being rejected, put off, and put down, and when we decide to try to stretch ourselves in how we try to communicate the love of Christ, we are going to get shot at from both sides. There is a lot of risk, danger, and work associated with this kind of ministry, and it is not for the faint of heart!

And so it isn't. But many Christians, including clergy, will find outreach to the unchurched more interesting and challenging than merely caring for Christians and managing the circulation of the saints. If the same old church routine doesn't pump your adrenalin or drive you to your knees anymore, a mission to the unchurched will! The people of one church got involved with starting a new church in another part of their city. Following Norm Whan's "The Phone's For You" program, they telephoned over 20,000 households, saw over 200 people at the new church's first service and, a few months later, saw over 100 new believers join the new church as charter members. When they returned to "First Church," they were different people. They had contracted "apostolic fever!" They presented their pastor with a "problem": they would serve on no more committees, nor do any more "ecclesiastical chores." They would now invest their lives in their congregation's mission to unchurched people.

That same kind of discovery is happening often enough, in enough places, to forecast the apostolic renaissance of mainsteam Christianity in the western world. While Christendom is gone with the wind and the Church no longer has the home field advantage, a growing number of christian groups and churches are becoming like the Notre Dame football team—who relish the challenge of playing the game on the other team's field! Notre Dame does not always win on "enemy turf," but they are energized by that challenge to their commitment, community, and comradeship more than by playing at home!

To be sure, the challenge Christians face in a secular world is more serious than anything Notre Dame ever faces in the Orange Bowl. We are called to mission in a fallen world, whose kingdoms are not yet the Kingdom of our God and of Christ, a world in which evil sometimes seems to be in charge. Before we go, we are counseled to wait until we "have been clothed with power from on high" (Luke 24:49). As we go, we remember that God's prevenient grace precedes us and that "the one who is in you is greater than the one who is in the world" (1 John 4:4).

N O T E S

INTRODUCTION: HOW THE WEST WAS LOST

1. G. M. Trevelyan, *English Social History* (New York: Longman Inc., 1978) p. 42.

2. Lesslie Newbigin, *Foolishness to the Greeks: The Gospel and Western Culture* (Grand Rapids: William B. Eerdmans, 1986) p. 129.

3. At the height of Christendom, the Church controlled a third of the lands of France and Germany, a fourth of the land of Great Britain, and much of the other lands of Europe.

4. Alan Walker, *Standing Up to Preach* (Nashville: Discipleship Resources, 1983) p. 16.

5. Ibid.

6. See Ralph Winter's address at the 1974 Lausanne Congress on World Evangelization, "The Highest Priority: Cross-cultural Evangelism," in J. D. Douglas, ed., *Let the Earth Hear His Voice* (Minneapolis: World Wide Publications, 1975) pp. 213-25.

7. The first influential definition of secularization was offered by C. A. van Peursen (in a widely influential Consultation, in 1959, at the Ecumenical Institute at Bossey, Switzerland): "Secularization means deliverance first from religious and then from metaphysical control over human reason and language." Peter Berger, in *The Sacred Canopy* (Garden City, N.Y.: Doubleday, 1969) p. 107, defined secularization as "the process by which sectors of society and culture are removed from the domination of religious institutions and symbols." More recently, Wolfhart Pannenberg sees secularization referring simply to "the way in which the world of culture has become independent from Christianity and above all from the churches" (*Christianity in a Secularized World* [New York: Crossroad, 1989] p. vii). This range of definitions represents the turf and shows that, consistently, some church leaders have been conceptualizing the Church's new challenge in the West for over 30 years; Lesslie Newbigin's *Foolishness to the Greeks: The Gospel and Western Culture* (cited in note 2 above) was *not*, as some people suppose, the first trumpet calling the Church to see this part of its mission. Furthermore, communicators like John Wesley and William Booth were effectively tackling this challenge before it had yet been named or diagnosed.

8. The complete Reformation event includes, of course, the Roman Catholic Counter-Reformation that sent unprecedented numbers of mission-

aries to other peoples, a dimension of the recovery of the ancient apostolic tradition which the Protestant Churches were not to recover for two centuries. Catholics made propaganda use of Protestantism's neglect of mission, contending that the Protestant Churches were not true churches, because they lacked the fourth sign of the True Church—"Apostolic." The reasons for Protestant Christianity's neglect of mission is partly mysterious, but Luther and Calvin appear to have concluded that the Great Commission was intended for the original generation of apostles only, and they fulfilled it.

9. See Peter Gay, *A Godless Jew: Freud, Atheism, and the Making of Psychoanalysis* (New Haven: Yale University Press, 1987).

10. Remarkably, Enlightenment thinkers assumed that reason would confirm traditional western morality—which, largely, had come from the Church.

11. But other Enlightenment thinkers experienced a secularization of God consciousness. For instance, Adam Smith and Karl Marx both perceived an ultimate force shaping history. Adam Smith advocated the free marketplace's "Invisible Hand" working through everyone's self-interest for the corporate good of all; for Marx the ultimate force was a Dialectical Process moving history toward the promised classless society.

12. Some writers identify still other causes of western secularization; David Edwards, for instance, identifies the rise of the great European universities as secularizing forces in western culture.

Some writers function from more of a "single cause" theory of secularization. Lesslie Newbigin regards the Enlightenment as the one great cause of secularization. Wolfhart Pannenberg advances the exotic, but plausible, theory that when European nationalism and the Reformation catalyzed a period of "confessional" wars and civil wars, some of western culture's influential opinion leaders, such as Hugo Grotius and Lord Herbert, concluded that Christianity no longer provided sufficient glue to hold western society and transnational brotherhood together peacefully; so they invented another religion—a "natural religion" in the hearts of all people (with "natural law" as a corollary), of which the historical religions are particular expressions, with cosmetic differences. As this doctrine was spread, Christianity was relativized in many minds, and consequently lost more of its influential role in western culture. In time, religion became optional for people, a matter of private preference. (See Pannenberg, cited in note 7 above, especially chapter one.)

13. As quoted in David Edwards, *The Futures of Christianity* (London: Hodder and Stoughton, 1987) p. 295.

14. Ibid., chapter 6, "In Secular Europe."

15. Martin Marty, *The Modern Schism: Three Paths to the Secular* (London: SCM Press, 1969).

16. R. H. Tawney, *Religion and the Rise of Capitalism* (Harmondsworth, England: Penguin Books, Ltd., 1922).

17. Søren Kierkegaard, *Attack Upon Christendom*, trans. by Walter Lowrie (Princeton, N.J.: Princeton University Press, 1944).

18. Rudolf Bultmann, "New Testament and Mythology," in *Kerygma and Myth*, ed. by Hans-Werner Bartsch, trans. by R. H. Fuller (London: SPCK, 1961).

19. Dietrich Bonhoeffer, *Letters and Papers from Prison* (New York: Macmillan, 1953). Bonhoeffer believed that Bultmann's "demythologizing" did not go far enough, because the problem with "man come of age" is not merely outmoded mythological conceptions but religious conceptions themselves!

20. Within this "private" world, the culture assumes that nothing is "wrong" except regarding someone else's belief, value, or life-style as wrong.

21. "Dr. Soper Outlines Christian Witness Plans," *The Methodist Recorder* (Jan. 15, 1953).

22. Donald Soper, "Viewpoint: Lord Soper on Contemporary Evangelism," *The Methodist Recorder* (Sept. 9, 1967). Soper adds that because of the Church's new apostolic environment, "authoritarian forms of evangelism" will be counterproductive—impressing gullible people but repelling thoughtful people. A "reasonable presentation" of Christianity "must come before the appeal, and must not be scamped as a minor stage in the process."

23. To be sure, the christian movement does not need to begin from scratch in most of the western world. If the five typical stages of mission are (1) the exploratory stage, (2) the mission station stage, (3) the stage of national leadership, (4) the indigenous stage, and (5) the stage of wider expansion, then in most of the West we are clearly past the exploratory and mission station stages, and most churches are self-governing and self-supporting—in the hands of national leaders. But there are many subcultures in which there is little or no viable christian presence, and often where we are past the first three stages, those churches are not culturally indigenous to the undiscipled populations, and are not working at the wider evangelism for which they are positioned.

24. Diogenes Allen, *Christian Belief in a Postmodern World: The Full Wealth of Conviction* (Louisville: Westminster/John Knox Press, 1989). My discussions of the Enlightenment and the rise of a "post-modern age" are indebted to, but not restricted to, Diogenes Allen's splendid contribution. Professor Allen is by no means a lone voice announcing the Enlightenment's demise. George A Lindbeck, professor of theology at Yale, is charting theology's course in the emerging "post-liberal age" (See *The Nature of Doctrine: Religion and Theology in a Postliberal Age* [Philadelphia: Westminster Press, 1984]. Thomas C. Oden delineates a similar agenda in *After Modernity. . . What? Agenda for Theology* (Grand Rapids: Zondervan, 1990). Charles H. Kraft, in *Christianity with Power* (Servant Books, 1989) chapter 4, contends that the liberal wing of the Church was co-opted by the Enlightenment and bought its assumptions; "Enlightenment Christianity" lacks the supernatural power found in original Christianity.

25. See Donald O. Soper, *Calling for Action: An Autobiographical Inquiry* (London: Robson Books, 1984) chapter 16.

CHAPTER 1: PROFILING THE SECULAR POPULATION

1. See J. Russell Hale, *The Unchurched: Who They Are and Why They Stay Away* (San Francisco: Harper & Row, 1980). The types of unchurched who are preponderantly secular are 1) The "Anti-institutionalists," who see churches competing with each other to build, or protect, their own empires; 2) The "Boxed-in," who resist being controlled by doctrines, ethics, people, and leaders; 3) The "Hedonists," who idolize leisure pursuits; 4) "The Locked Out"—the rejected, neglected, or discriminated populations who feel unwanted by the churches; 5) The "Pilgrims," who view all knowledge as incomplete; 6) The "Publicans," who are critical of hypocrisy in the churches; 7) The "True Unbelievers," who are the five percent of the population who are conscious atheists, agnostics, deists, etc. Hale's other three types of unchurched people are: 1) The "Burned Out," who once got overcommitted and consumed in a church; they graduated, and said "never again." 2) The "Floaters," who move from one church to another, refraining from deep involvement with any church. 3) The "Nomads," who change residence often and attend church wherever they live, but avoid deep involvement now to avoid grief later. Most people in these three groups are exposed to enough Christianity to understand it; many would count themselves as "believers" but not "belongers."

2. See Kenneth Chafin, *The Reluctant Witness* (Nashville: Broadman Press, 1974) chapter 6.

3. Reginald Bibby, *Fragmented Gods: The Poverty and Potential of Religion in Canada* (Toronto: Irwin Publishing, 1987) chapters 3–4.

4. Ibid., p. 82.

5. The philosopher Michael Polanyi presented a contrasting view of secular society as characterized by a "moral inversion," with two features: 1) Many people fear "hypocrisy" and value "honesty," with the result that some people live a "unholier-than-thou" life-style, assuming it is better to live honestly from low motives than from high motives one may not always attain! 2) But at a deeper level, modern secular society has experienced "the outbreak of a moral fervor which has achieved numberless humanitarian reforms and has improved modern society beyond the boldest thoughts of earlier centuries. . . . This fervor . . . in our own lifetime has outreached itself by its inordinate aspirations and thus heaped on mankind the disasters that have befallen us." See Drusilla Scott, *Everyman Revived: The Common Sense of Michael Polanyi* (Chippenham, England: Antony Rowe Ltd. 1986) p. 98.

6. Lesslie Newbigin, *Foolishness to the Greeks: The Gospel and Western Culture* (cited in note 2 of the Introduction).

7. The term "reflective practitioners" was popularized by Donald A. Schon's excellent book on professionalism, *The Reflective Practitioner: How Professionals Think in Action* (New York: Basic Books, Inc., 1983). Some academic fields, such as management and psychotherapy, regularly draw insight from the reflections of its pioneering practitioners, but this is largely a foreign method for theology (although John Wesley's field experiences in ministry helped inform his ministry and theology), and, except for pastoral counseling, pastoral theology, and church growth, is not yet widely used in the other fields informing ministries and mission.

8. Alan Walker, *The Whole Gospel for the Whole World* (New York-Nashville: Abingdon Press, 1957) pp. 29-30.

9. Donald O. Soper, *The Advocacy of the Gospel* (New York-Nashville: Abingdon Press, 1961) p. 14.

10. In Alan Walker, *A Ringing Call to Mission* (New York-Nashville: Abingdon Press, 1966) pp. 14-16.

11. Soper, *The Advocacy of the Gospel*, p. 18.

12. As quoted in ibid., p. 18.

13. Ibid., p. 19.

14. Ibid.

15. "Donald Soper on Preaching to Doubters." *The Methodist Recorder* (May 24, 1962).

16. Donald Soper, *Calling for Action: An Autobiographical Inquiry* (cited in note 25 of the Introduction) pp. 9-10.

17. Helmut Thielicke, *The Trouble with the Church* (New York: Harper and Row, 1965) pp. 1-11.

18. The first three of these points were suggested in Soper's 1971 address, "What I Have Learned About Communicating with the Outsider," later published in Harold Bales, ed., *Bridges to the World* (Nashville: Tidings, 1971) pp. 42-54.

19. Robert Schuller, *Believe in the God Who Believes in You* (Nashville: Thomas Nelson Publishers, 1989) p. 36.

20. Ibid., pp. 41-43.

21. See the Introduction to Schuller's *Believe in the God Who Believes in You,* and also Schuller's *Your Church Has a Fantastic Future* (Ventura, Calif.: Regal Books, 1986) pp. 106-7.

22. From *Self-Esteem: The New Reformation* (Waco: Word Books, 1982) p. 156.

23. See *Believe in the God Who Believes in You,* chapter 2.

24. Shoemaker observes, for instance, in *How to Become a Christian* (New York: Harper & Row, 1953) chapter 3, that "there are thousands in this world who do not get drunk on alcohol, but they get very drunk on fear and self-pity and depression and a desire to have their own way in life. A man who returns home in a cantankerous mood in the evening, a woman determined to use her ailments as a way of getting attention and service, are both drunk—one on moods, the other on self-centeredness."

25. Quoted in Samuel Shoemaker, *Extraordinary Living for Ordinary Men* (Grand Rapids: Zondervan, 1965) p. 24.

26. Helen Smith Shoemaker's biography, *I Stand By the Door: The Life of Sam Shoemaker* (Waco: Word Books, 1978) begins with the full poem.

CHAPTER 2: THEMES AND STRATEGIES FOR REACHING SECULAR PEOPLE

1. Donald O. Soper, *Popular Fallacies About the Christian Faith* (London: The Epworth Press, 1938; rpt. by Wyvern Books, 1957) p. 124.

2. Michael Bennett, *Christianity Explained* (Singapore: Scripture Union, 1988).

3. Samuel Shoemaker, *Children of the Second Birth* (New York: Fleming H. Revell Company, 1927) pp. 87-89.

4. Dean M. Kelley, *Why Conservative Churches Are Growing* (New York: Harper & Row, 1977). See especially chapter 3, "The Indispensable Function of Religion."

5. David Robinson, of the United Church of Australia's Board of Mission, shared a dialogical approach in a seminar at Lausanne II in Manila that looks widely useful. You ask 1) "What occupies your mind?" They typically refer to their health, anxieties, work, marriage, or children. You ask 2) "What does this uncertainty mean?" You suggest that the Bible has some answers to their struggles; they usually want to know what it says. 3) It is often necessary, and liberating, to get them to *name* their enemy: "My enemy is. . . ." Sometimes they ask "What if I don't believe in the Bible?" Robinson encourages them to "Just read it, and be open to God; make up your own mind in time."

6. "Donald Soper on Preaching to Doubters," *The Methodist Recorder* (May 24, 1962).

7. Donald Morgan, *How to Get It Together When Your World Is Coming Apart* (Old Tappan, N. J.: Fleming H. Revell, 1988).

8. Samuel Shoemaker, *Children of the Second Birth* (cited in note 3, chapter 2) p. 13.

9. Ibid., pp. 35-42.

10. Ibid., pp. 51-58.

11. See Donald Soper's *Question Time on Tower Hill* (London: Hodder and Stoughton Ltd., 1935) pp. 21-23. The full passage expands Soper's understanding of the role of fellowship in both the loss of faith and the discovery of faith: "A loss of confidence in the Church of God has resulted in a corresponding doubt [about] God. Beginning with a distrust of the . . . Church's leaders, multitudes have ceased to believe in the spiritual realities to which those leaders were . . . witnesses. . . . The disillusionment with the institution came first and doubt [about] the reality behind the institution . . . followed. The majority of those who no longer call

themselves Christians did not lose their faith in God and therefore cease to find any usefulness in Churches. . . .

"The decay of faith is the direct outcome of the decay of fellowship. Private atheism is only very rarely the result of private study; in most instances it is the outcome of moral disillusionment with public worship and corporate Christianity. Only in a vital Christian fellowship will God become real to most people. [Private] mysticism is not the broad highway of Christian experience. . . . The key to the problem of modern day agnosticism is fellowship. Out of the failure of Christian fellowship it has emerged, and in the recovery of a Christian fellowship it will give place once again to faith and assurance."

12. Robert H. Schuller, *Self-Esteem: The New Reformation* (cited in note 22 of chapter 1) p. 156.

13. See George G. Hunter III, *To Spread the Power: Church Growth in the Wesleyan Spirit* (Nashville: Abingdon Press, 1987) for expansions of each of the following five principles.

14. Kenneth Chafin, *The Reluctant Witness* (cited in note 2, chapter 1) p. 19.

15. Ibid., pp. 26-27.

16. Kenneth Chafin, *Help! I'm a Layman* (Waco: Word Books, 1966) p. 38.

17. Ibid., p. 107.

18. See Eugene Nida's splendid article, "Dynamics of Church Growth," in *Church Growth and Christian Mission*, ed. Donald A. McGavran (Pasadena, Calif.: William Carey Library, 1976).

19. Quoted in Bruce Larson, *Ask Me to Dance* (Waco: Word Books, 1972) pp. 10-11.

20. Donald Soper, *Calling for Action: An Autobiographical Inquiry* (cited in note 25 of the introduction) p. 10.

21. The series, preached at South Main Baptist Church in Houston and to a regional television audience, has not yet been published. But Chafin's book, *How to Know When You've Got It Made* (Waco: Word Books, 1981) reflects some of these insights from David's life.

22. Shoemaker's full poem "I Stand By the Door: An Apologia for My Life" is printed in his biography (cited in note 26 of chapter 1) pp. ix-x.

CHAPTER 3: COMMUNICATING WITH SECULAR PEOPLE

1. See the first chapter of Charles G. Finney's *Lectures on Revivals of Religion*, ed. William G. McLoughlin (Cambridge: Harvard University Press, 1960), and published in many other editions over the last century and a half.

2. The product of Augustine's own "plundering" is his text *On Christian*

Doctrine (De Doctrina Christiana), trans. D. W. Robertson, Jr., Library of Liberal Arts (Indianapolis: Bobbs-Merrill, 1958). This lecture series represents Augustine's adaptation of Ciceronian rhetoric—the most sophisticated communication theory then available, for the christian preacher and teacher. The book became the most influential communication text for Christians for almost one thousand years!

3. See Aristotle. *The Rhetoric of Aristotle* trans., Lane Cooper (Englewood Cliffs, N. J.: Prentice-Hall, 1960). An excellent modern text in Aristotle's tradition is Edward P. J. Corbett, *Classical Rhetoric for the Modern Student*, 3rd ed. (New York-Oxford: Oxford University Press, 1990).

4. Aristotle has, of course, been "improved upon" in the last 23 centuries; the several traditions of communication studies have expanded upon his understanding of all three components. Augustine saw, in *De Doctrina Christiana*, that the communicator's actual character is important in communication, not merely the audience's perception of the communicator's character. Stephen Toulmin's "layout" of an argument advances our knowledge beyond Aristotle's model of deduction. Disciplines like linguistics and general semantics advance our useful knowledge of effective language in communication. The behavioral sciences advance our ability to understand audiences and various sociocultural contexts for communicaion.

Furthermore, the several disciplines that inform communication theory today have added considerably to the known *dynamics* of communication. We now perceive communication to be less of a single speech event than Aristotle did, and more of a (mysterious) "process." Communication is not as linear as Aristotle presupposed, but involves more of a "circular" two way dialogue over time. We now more greatly stress the communication of "meaning," and not just the transmission of content. We now know that effective communication is often at least as much "relational" as it is content transmission. We know that communication may be intentional—as Aristotle presupposed, but it may take place unintentionally. And we now know that effective communication can even take place across cultures, if the communicator can adapt the message's forms to fit the receiver's culture.

Likewise, we are now aware of *components* in the communication process beyond Aristotle's three factors of source, message, and receiver. We know that the "source" may be perceived to be a group, movement, or institution—like the government or the Church, and not merely the particular spokesman. We know that the communicator begins with a meaning that he or she wants to stimulate in the receiver; that the communicator "encodes" a message—based in part upon knowledge, or assumptions, of the receiver's subject knowledge, attitudes, needs, culture, etc. We know that the message is transmitted over one or more "channels," that the message experiences "entropy," i.e., loss or distortion in the process of its transmission, and that the message is subjected to "noise," i.e., disruptive factors ranging from static in the channel, to ambiguity in the symbols, to distractions in the environment; all of which argues for "redundancy," i.e., creative repetition in communicating the message. We know that the receiver brings to the transaction a "filter" developed from years of enculturation and experiences, through which he or she receives and "decodes" the message before deciding what the message "means." We know that the receiver is apprehending messages from the communicator's language *and* from the communicator's various nonverbal "paralinguistic" messages. We know that the receiver may give "feedback," verbally and/or nonverbally, to the original communicator—which enables the communicator to adjust the message for greater effectiveness. We know that the immediate occasion and setting, with its symbols, influences the receivers expectations before the transaction and influences the later response. We know that, generally, more effective communicators function with an awareness of all or most of these known communication dynamics and components and that, generally, less effective communicators function with an awareness of fewer of the known dynamics and components.

The most enduring modern text applying communication theory to christian mission and evangelization is Eugene A. Nida, *Message and Mission: The Communication of the Christian Faith*, rev. ed. (Pasadena, Calif.: William Carey Library, 1990).

5. Chafin, *The Reluctant Witness* (cited in note 2 of chapter 1) p. 127.

6. See Everett M. Rogers, *Diffusion of Innovations,* 3rd ed. (New York: Free Press, 1983).

7. "There Is No Mass Evangelism," *British Weekly* CXXXII (May 8, 1952) p. 1.

8. Ibid.

9. Quoted in Isabel Baumgartner, "The Lord's Barnstormer," *The Episcopalian* (Sept. 1963) p. 38.

10. Bryan Green, *The Practice of Evangelism* (New York: Charles Scribner's Sons, 1951) pp. 81-82.

11. Ibid., pp. 27-29.

12. Ibid., p. 27.

13. Bryan S. W. Green, "Evangelism and the Young," *The Expository Times* LVIII (1946) p. 32.

14. Lesslie Newbigin, *Foolishness to the Greeks: The Gospel and Western Culture* (cited in note 2 of the Introduction) pp. 1-11.

15. Ibid., p. 7.

16. For a full explanation, see Donald A. McGavran, *Understanding Church Growth*, third edition, rev. and ed. by C. Peter Wagner (Grand Rapids: William B. Eerdmans, 1990) chapter 13.

17. See the excellent study by Leslie Paul, *The Deployment and Payment of the Clergy* (Westminster, England: W. & J. MacKay & Co. Ltd., 1963).

18. I should add that Mr. Wesley also functioned on his own biblical understanding of key theological terms. *Salvation* was essentially salvation from the power of sin in one's life, even more than preparing one's soul for heaven. Salvation is experienced through *faith*, which, though faith is

informed by the orthodox doctrine, is more personal trust in God than mere assent to orthodox opinions. A *Christian* is a person who has experienced the love of God and acceptance by God, and who now lives a new life, by the grace mediated in the faith community, which enables him or her to do the will of God and do good to all people, motivated by love, seeking both personal and social righteousness in this life (see Wesley's classic essay "The Character of a Methodist").

19. A class functioned as a "gymnasium" of the human spirit, in which class members helped each other to live as Christians. The christian life was made normative in terms of three vows: to live one's life 1) doing good, 2) avoiding evil, and 3) exposing one's soul to the means of grace. A weekly meeting essentially consisted of each person reporting on his or her performance that week vis-à-vis the three vows, with each person's peers responding, as appropriate, with affirmation and celebration, or challenge and rebuke.

20. The truth, relevance, and stimulation versions of the Image barrier, together, do not exhaust the versions of this outermost barrier, but they illustrate the complexity of a secular audience, and they show why there is no "quick fix," no shortcut to getting to know people, no substitute for beginning where they are.

21. Not all secular people who do consider the gospel will accept it. For instance, some people will not accept what Bonhoeffer called "the cost of discipleship." Others will find a gospel of grace difficult to accept in a culture that values self-reliance. William A. Dyrness, in *How Does America Hear the Gospel?* (Grand Rapids: William B. Eerdmans, 1989), amplifies this point: "Individualism in our modern sense of self-sufficiency seems more closely related to the attempt of Adam and Eve to be their own gods. The self-realizing, self-defining individual too often becomes a barrier to hearing the cries of his neighbor or obeying the voice of God" (p. 103).

22. See "Power: Preaching for Total Commitment," chapter 9 in Bill Hybels, Stuart Briscoe, and Haddon Robinson, eds., *Mastering Contemporary Preaching* (Portland: Multnomah Press, 1989).

23. Ibid., pp. 114-15.

24. Bruce Larson, *Setting Men Free* (Grand Rapids: Zondervan, 1967) p. 34.

25. Alan Walker, *The Whole Gospel for the Whole World* (New York-Nashville, Abingdon Press, 1957) p. 59.

26. Ibid., pp. 59-60.

27. James A. Harnish, *Jesus Makes the Difference! The Gospel in Human Experience* (Nashville: The Upper Room, 1987) chapter 2, "Confessions of a Workaholic."

28. "The Agents of Change in '89," *The Lexington Herald-Leader* (Dec. 30, 1989) Section C, p. 2.

29. Bruce Larson, *Ask Me to Dance* (cited in note 19, chapter 2) p. 111.

30. Bruce Larson, *Setting Men Free* (cited above in note 24) p. 41.

31. Harnish, *Jesus Makes the Difference!* (cited above in note 27) pp. 100-101.

32. See Samuel M. Shoemaker, *The Experiment of Faith: A Handbook for Beginners* (New York: Harper and Bros., 1957) especially chapter five, "How to Work for Christ Through Your Job."

33. J. Russell Hale, *The Unchurched: Who They Are and Why They Stay Away* (cited in note 1 of chapter 1) p. 184.

34. Ibid., p. 183.

35. David Womack, *The Pyramid Principle of Church Growth* (Bethany Fellowship Inc., 1977) pp. 64-65.

36. Green, *The Practice of Evangelism* (cited in note 10 of chapter 3) p. 79, and an unpublished lecture on "Dealing with Individuals."

37. Donald Morgan, *How to Get It Together When Your World Is Coming Apart* (cited in note 7 of chapter 2) pp. 127-28.

38. See James Harnish's *Jesus Makes the Difference!* (Nashville: The Upper Room, 1987) chapter 3, "When Tragedy Strikes."

39. Quoted in Donald Morgan, *How to Get It Together When Your World Is Coming Apart*, p.18.

40. Bruce Larson, *Setting Men Free* (cited above in note 24) p. 43.

41. Hybels, Briscoe, and Robinson, "Power: Preaching for Total Commitment" (cited in note 22 of chapter 3) p. 120.

42. Ibid.

43. William Warren Sweet, *Revivalism in America* (New York-Nashville: Abingdon Press, 1944) p. xii.

44. Green, "There Is No Mass Evangelism" (cited in note 7 of chapter 3), p. 2. Emphasis added.

45. Bill Hybels, "Speaking to the Secular Mind," *Leadership* (Summer 1988) p. 32.

CHAPTER 4: WHAT KIND OF CHRISTIANS REACH SECULAR PEOPLE?

1. "Dr. Soper Outlines Christian Witness Plans," *The Methodist Recorder* (Jan. 15, 1953).

2. S. M. Shoemaker, Jr., *Children of the Second Birth* (cited in note 3, chapter 2) p. 11.

3. This introduces a curious paradox in the western Church. David J. Bosch, in chapter 9 of *Transforming Mission: Paradigm Shifts in Theology of Mission* (Maryknoll, NY: Orbis Books, 1991), demonstrates that Protestant Christianity's unprecedented involvement in foreign missions to the Third World in the last two centuries is, in several ways, a large scale response to the Enlightenment. This makes Protestant Christianity's blindness to the post-Enlightenment mission fields of Europe and North America, and the Church's business-as-usual agenda in the West, all the more remarkable.

4. From William Barclay, *The Master's Men* (Nashville: Abingdon Press, 1959).

5. Alan Walker wrote of the rationale and early development of Life Line in *As Close As the Telephone* (Nashville-New York: Abingdon Press, 1967). A later account is in his *Caring for the World: The Continuing Story of the Life Line Christian Telephone Ministries* (Glasgow: Collins/Fount Paperbacks, 1979). In chapter four, Walker makes the case for the indispensable christian identity of this lay counseling ministry. In his book *How Jesus Helped People* (Nashville-New York: Abingdon Press, 1964) Walker shares the biblical material that has helped inform this worldwide lay ministry. See also *Standing Up to Preach* (Nashville: Discipleship Resources, 1983) p. 28. Because another organization "owned" the "Lifeline" name in the United States, this ministry in the United States is "Contact Telephone Ministries," and was pioneered by Ross Whetstone.

6. Walker, *As Close As the Telephone*, p. 56. See also Walker, *A Ringing Call to Mission* (cited in note 10, chapter 1) chapter 8, "The Atomic Power of the Laity."

7. From Alan Walker, chapter 8: "The Task of the Laity" in *The Whole Gospel for the Whole World* (New York-Nashville: Abingdon Press, 1957) pp. 85-94.

8. Chafin, *The Reluctant Witness* (cited in note 2 of chapter 1) p. 42.

9. Quoted in Walker, *A Ringing Call to Mission* (cited in note 10, chapter 1) p. 116.

10. Quoted in Lester Thonssen, A. Craig Baird, and Waldo W. Braden, *Speech Criticism*, 2nd ed. (New York: The Ronald Press Company, 1970) p. 445.

11. Donald O. Soper, *Popular Fallacies About the Christian Faith* (cited in note 1, chapter 2) pp. 120-21. Soper adds: " 'Woe is me if I preach not the gospel' is not the somewhat extravagant cry of the fanatic: *it is the one supreme condition of evangelism.* When I am utterly persuaded of the truth and power of the faith I hold, then everything will be laid under contribution to its demand. My mind, my desires, my habits, my life itself will all be harnessed to this consuming purpose. The truth of the saw that religion is 'caught not taught' lies here, and the remarkable effects produced by the preaching of John Wesley, for example, are hard to believe just by reading his sermons; they only become credible when we appreciate the intensity of passion which burnt in the heart of the man who delivered them."

12. Alan Walker, *Standing Up to Preach: The Art of Evangelical Preaching* (cited in note 5 above) p. 78. For a fuller treatment of Walker's third-person emphasis see his *Breakthrough: Rediscovery of the Holy Spirit* (Atlanta: Lay Renewal Publications, 1969).

13. Bryan Green, *The Practice of Evangelism* (cited in note 10 of chapter 3) p. 20.

14. Ibid., p. 7.

15. Samuel M. Shoemaker, *The Experiment of Faith* (cited note 32 of chapter 3) p. 12.

16. Ibid., p. 23.

17. Ibid., p. 26.

18. Samuel Shoemaker, *Extraordinary Living for Ordinary Men* (cited in note 25, chapter 1) p. 28.

19. Samuel Shoemaker, *The Practice of Evangelism* (cited in note 10 of chapter 3) p. 25.

20. For expansion on this important insight see the books by William Muehl, *All the Damned Angels* (Toronto: United Church Press, 1972) and *Why Preach? Why Listen?* (Philadelphia: Fortress Press, 1986).

21. In the Introduction to Samuel Shoemaker, *Extraordinary Living for Ordinary Men* (cited in note 25, chapter 1).

22. Robert H. Schuller, *Self-esteem: The New Reformation* (cited in note 12, chapter 2) pp. 159-60.

23. Alan Walker, *Standing Up to Preach* (cited in note 5 above) pp. 35-36.

24. Donald Soper, "Challenge to the Church," *The Daily Herald* (Jan. 11, 1937).

25. In Bruce Larson, *Ask Me to Dance* (cited in note 19, chapter 2) p. 32.

26. G. K. Chesterton, *Orthodoxy* (Image Books, 1959) pp. 107ff.

27. Bruce Larson, *Ask Me to Dance*, pp. 35-36. The whole of chapter three focuses on this challenge.

28. Donald Soper, *Tower Hill 12:30* (London: Epworth Press, 1963) chapter 5.

29. Samuel M. Shoemaker, *How to Become a Christian* (cited in note 24, chapter 1).

30. Donald Soper, *Tower Hill, 12:30*, p. 70.

CHAPTER 5: WHAT KIND OF CHURCH REACHES SECULAR PEOPLE?

1. Bruce Larson and Ralph Osborne, *The Emerging Church* (Waco: Word Books, 1970).

2. Ibid., p. 11

3. Ibid., pp. 16-17.

4. Ibid., p. 27.

5. Ibid., chapter 2.

6. Bruce Larson and Ralph Osborne, *No Longer Strangers* (Waco: Word Books, 1976).

7. Bruce Larson and Ralph Osborne, *The Relational Revolution* (Waco: Word Books, 1976).

8. Larson and Osborne, *No Longer Strangers,* p. 63.

9. Ibid., p. 70, emphasis added.

10. Larson and Osborne, *The Emerging Church,* p. 33.

11. Larson and Osborne, *No Longer Strangers,* p. 83, emphasis added.

12. Larson and Osborne, *The Emerging Church*, p. 34.

13. Larson and Osborne, *No Longer Strangers*, p. 94.

14. Ibid., chapter 7.

15. I would add that our Lord has much to teach us about the gospel through our sharing it with people who do not yet believe. In his remarkable book, *Christianity Rediscovered* (Chicago: Orbis Books, 1978), Vincent Donovan tells the story of his 16 years of itinerant apostolic ministry among Masai tribes of East Africa—work which resulted in two achievements: (1) the planting of an indigenous Masai Catholic Church, and (2) Donovan's own "rediscovery" of Christianity in greater depth and wider relevance than he had ever imagined. This is the testimony of every christian witness who takes a nonformula approach and works out the gospel's meaning *with* people: that they discover new richness in the gospel as they see its impact in the other person and join them in reflecting upon their experiences of grace.

16. Larson and Osborne, *No Longer Strangers*, pp. 18-20, 26.

17. Ibid., p. 21.

18. Larson and Osborne, *The Emerging Church*, p. 70.

19. Larson, *Setting Men Free* (cited in note 24, chapter 3) in the foreword.

20. And with indebtedness to J. C. Hoekendijk, *The Church Inside Out* (Philadelphia: Westminster Press, 1966).

21. Reflection upon my data from converts and congregations leads me to depart somewhat from this shorthand version of the triad. This working version may leave the impression that life-changing faith comes only when Christ meets people through the verbalized gospel, spoken or written. But in the Scripture, Christ also meets us where "two or more" are gathered in His name, and He also meets us through ministry to people in need (Matthew 25). Furthermore, my career interviews with converts have surfaced many first-generation believers who met Christ *first* in a fellowship—reminding me that the faith is as much "caught" as "taught"; and some converts first met Christ, say, while protesting an injustice, or serving a social cause, or building a home with Habitat for Humanity. Occasional converts report meeting Christ while involved in a cross-cultural mission program; but during the program, their exposure to the Scripture and the fellowship-in-mission were indispensable in making sense of what they were experiencing, so all three expressions of the gospel contributed to their conversion. So Christ meets people, enables their new birth, and confers and shapes their faith through kerygma *and* koinonia *and* diakonia; it does not matter which of these engages them first, but all three must engage them in time. I first developed some of this material in *The Contagious Congregation: Frontiers in Evangelism and Church Growth* (Nashville: Abingdon Press, 1979) pp. 28-34.

22. "Evangelism in the 70s," in John R. Bisagno, Kenneth L. Chafin, C. Wake Freeman and others, *How to Win Them* (Nashville: Broadman Press, 1970) pp. 26-27.

23. See Abraham H. Maslow, *Motivation and Personality* (New York: Harper & Row, 1970) chapters 3-4.

24. See chapter one of Larson's *Setting Men Free* (cited in note 24 of chapter 3).

25. Larson and Osborne, *The Emerging Church*, chapters 5 and 6.

26. Ibid., chapter 10, p. 151.

27. Ibid., p. 93.

28. Ibid, pp. 94-100.

29. Ibid, p. 100.

30. Bill Hybels, *Honest to God? Becoming an Authentic Christian* (Grand Rapids: Zondervan, 1990) p. 125.

31. Kelley, *Why Conservative Churches Are Growing* (cited in note 4, chapter 2).

32. Bill Hybels, "Speaking to the Secular Mind" (cited in note 45, chapter 3) pp. 29-30.

33. Ibid., p. 30.

34. Quoted in the "Suburban Living" section of the *Chicago Daily Herald* (May 18, 1988).

35. *Time* (March 6, 1989) p. 60.

36. From the Willow Creek audiotape, "Building a Church for the Unchurched." I have noted three particular differences in denominations starting many new congregations and those who do not. In growing denominations, new church planting is (1) an exciting dimension of the broader mission, (2) established local churches start new churches, and (3) they encourage entrepreneurial personalities to be founding pastors. In declining denominations (1) the judicatories are "assigned" the (2) "responsibility" of starting new churches, and the few new churches started that way are (3) often pastored by "good company men."

37. As an example of unchurched people's needs determining the church's programs, the Crystal Cathedral offers a great number of 12-Step support groups for people with various addictions. As an example of unchurched people's hangups determining the church's strategy, Schuller delivers a "message," *not* a "sermon." As an example of the unchurched people's culture determining the church's style, the church addresses problems and themes, and uses language and music, to which unchurched people can relate. Finally, the church's growth goals are determined by the number of unchurched people in the ministry area, not by some "ideal" size for the church to attain.

38. For more on a church's strategic planning process and how it enables church growth, see chapter 8 in Hunter, *To Spread the Power: Church Growth in the Wesleyan Spirit* (Nashville: Abingdon Press, 1987).

39. Summarized from the Bill Hybels tape, "The Seven-Step- Strategy of Willow Creek Church," available from the church's Seeds Tape Ministry Department, 67 East Algonquin Road, South Barrington, IL 60010. Telephone (708) 765-5000.

40. See John Ed Mathison, *Every Member in Ministry* (Nashville: Discipleship Resources, 1988) for this approach to lay ministry at Frazer Memorial UMC.

41. Chafin, *The Reluctant Witness* (cited in note 2, chapter 1) p. 141.

42. Bill Hybels's chapter on "Unstereotyping Evangelism," in *Honest to God? Becoming an Authentic Christian* (cited in note 30 above) chapter 10, summarizes Willow Creek's understanding of the motivation for evangelism and the mindset of the evangelist, as well as a description of these six biblical styles of evangelism. His four recorded messages on "Adventures in Personal Evangelism" are available from Willow Creek's Seeds Tape Ministry.

43. Hybels's five recorded messages on "Faith Has Its Reasons" are available for $12.00 from Willow Creek's Seeds Tape ministry. The five addresses, which present reasons for believing (1) in God, (2) in the Bible, (3) in Jesus Christ, (4) in the resurrection of Christ, and (5) in heaven and hell, represent the Willow Creek approach to the questions and doubts that secular seekers in their region ask.

44. Bill Hybels, "Speaking to the Secular Mind" (cited in note 45, chapter 3) p. 1.

45. Ibid., p 34.

46. From the *Chicago Daily Herald*, Suburban Living section (Thursday May 18, 1988).

47. See Hybels, "Power: Preaching for Total Commitment" (cited in note 22, chapter 3).

48. Ibid., pp. 114-15.

49. Ibid., pp. 119-20.

I N D E X

"multiple conversations" model of evangelism, 89-91
"multiplication of units" principle, 68-69
Muscle Beach, 11
music, role of in reaching secular people, 151-153

Nationalism, 27
natural religion, 28, 38, 174
Newbigin, Lesslie, 12, 35, 44, 47, 80-81
new congregations, importance of starting, 153-154
New Life for All movement, 87-88
Newton, Isaac, 27
Nida, Eugene, 68

Oden, Thomas, 91
Order of Salvation, John Wesley's, 81-83
Osborne, Ralph, 136-144

Pannenberg, Wolfhart, 173-74
pathos of the audience, 75
persistence, role of in apostolic ministry, 132-133
personalizing the message, 104
Polanyi, Michael, 176
possibilities of people, the, 123
proverbs, 105
psychology, 71-72

Rattenbury, J. Ernest, 46
receptive people, reaching, 64-65
relevance of Christianity, 47-48, 69-71, 76-79, 86
Reformation, The, 27, 173-74
relational theology, 137-40
religionless Christianity, 34
Renaissance, The, 26
research, role of in strategic evangelism, 124-25, 154-57, 166-67
Robinson, David, 56, 178

role models in apostolic ministry, 120-21
Russell, Bertrand, 30

"Saddleback Sam," 156
Saddleback Valley Community Church, 15, 69, 154-55, 158-60
Sayers, Dorothy, 96
Schuller, Robert, 13-14, 50-51, 61-62, 89, 97-98, 105, 127, 155
Schweitzer, Albert, 102
Science, 27-28
Seekers Service, Willow Creek, 165-68
Secularization: defined 25-26, 173; causes of 26-31; appraised 33-35; forms of 31-33; of other religions and worldviews, 32; of God-consciousness, 174
secular people; described, 11, 23, 41, 164; types of, 41; myths about, 42-43; characteristics of, 44-54; as lost and mattering to God, 53-54, 72, 144-45
Secularism, growth of 33
self-esteem, 51-52, 62-63
self-reliance, as a barrier to receiving grace, 103, 181
"Seven-Step Strategy" of Willow Creek Church, 159
Shoemaker, Samuel, 13-14, 45, 51-53, 56-57, 59-60, 72, 96-97, 108, 119, 121-22, 131-132, 177-78
small groups, 60, 63-64, 83, 144, 178-79, 181
social concerns and evangelism, 60-61, 139
social networks, outreach across, 65-66
Soper, Donald, 12, 36-37, 45-49, 55-56, 58, 60, 70, 107, 119-20, 125-27, 130, 132, 175, 178-79, 183
strategy and planning, 143-44, 158-59